The Complete Guide To
BUYING A CAFÉ

Practical Advice To Get It Right

Craig Reid

The Complete Guide To Buying A Café:
Practical Advice To Get It Right
Copyright © Craig Reid 2011
www.thecafeninja.com

The moral right of Craig Reid to be identified as
the author of this work has been asserted in accordance
with the Copyright Act 1968.

All rights reserved. No part of this publication may be reproduced
or transmitted by any means, electronic, photocopying or otherwise
without prior written permission of the author.

First published in Australia 2011 by The Publishing Queen
www.thepublishingqueen.com

ISBN 978-1-921673-53-5

Disclaimer
All information contained within this book constitutes general
advice only and is not in any way intended for any individual.
Should the reader choose to make use of the information contained
within, this is entirely their decision and the author, publisher and
their representatives do not assume any responsibility whatsoever
under any conditions or circumstances. Individuals should seek
their own professional advice applicable to their specific situation.

Information contained within regarding taxation issues is general
only and is based on taxation and planning systems applicable in
Australia. Readers elsewhere should seek professional advice
in their own region for specific information relevant to that country.

Any opinions expressed in this work are exclusively those of
the author and are not necessarily the views held or endorsed by
The Publishing Queen.

The Complete Guide To
BUYING A CAFÉ

Practical Advice To Get It Right

Craig Reid

Thank You

I would like to thank my wife, Romina for the continual prodding which has helped me to finally finish this book. Thanks also to my mother, Helen for her (unannounced, but quite amazing) proofreading skills, my father Bill for his ever-present financial knowledge, Violeta Balhas for her wonderful final edits and James from Klink for allowing us to take photos at his excellent café.

I would also like to thank all of my clients for their valuable feedback on their experiences of the buying process.

Thanks must also go to Robert Gerrish from the wonderful small business community *www.flyingsolo.com.au* not only for providing such an excellent resource for small business owners but for being kind enough to write a foreword for this book.

Last (and most definitely not least) I would like to thank my friend Robert Watson for continuing to motivate me to finish this book and for his incredibly detailed and thoroughly valuable editing and proofreading skills.

Foreword

When we wrote our book, *Flying Solo: How to go it alone in business* a few years ago, we explored the impact happiness has on business success and used the scenario of a café to get our point across. Would you give custom to a café that had grumpy staff? What's the atmosphere like in a café that's led by a miserable boss and would you want to spend time there?

Of course you wouldn't. Gloomy service businesses don't thrive.

What's more, I'll lay odds the cause of grumpiness is a business owner under stress and 10-1 that stress is caused by the business.

Our mythical café owner had not read *The Complete Guide To Buying A Café* by Craig Reid.

Through this insight-full book, Craig will not only help you avoid failure, but if you pay careful attention, he'll put you on a path to great prosperity.

I only wish Craig would write similar books for other industry sectors. Perhaps he will.

Devour every page of *The Complete Guide To Buying A Café* and be prepared to take notes.

Let me know when you open. But be warned I only drink espresso and am a keen advocate of the 'no crema, no serva' credo!

Love your work,

Robert Gerrish
Author, speaker, blogger and founder of
Flying Solo – Australia's micro business community

Contents

Introduction	11
Before You Start Looking For A Café	27
Finding A Café To Buy	39
Analysing The Business Summary	47
Analysing The Business Summary – An Example	69
Other Useful Information	105
Assessing The Location	115
Meeting The Owner	121
Analysis Techniques	151
The Trial & Settlement	163
A Day In The Life Of A Café Owner	173
About Craig Reid, The Café Ninja	190

Introduction

Your Dream

So you've decided to run your own business and for whatever reason, you already know what you want to do. Maybe you baked with granny in the kitchen when you were growing up, maybe you've always loved coffee, maybe you like dealing with people, maybe you just think that it looks cool. You want to run your own business, and that business is going to be a café. This level of passion is essential.

We, as human beings, tend to look for the sunshine in our lives, and if we don't have the sunshine, we look forward to better times when the clouds part and the silver lining is revealed. You are already looking up at the clouds at this stage and thinking of that silver lining...

What we've all dreamed of...

You will have time to choose your hours / days of work, shifts, etc. You will put in a hard day's work to run your business so that you can have a "better lifestyle" with less stress and more personal satisfaction in what you do. You will also earn more money, which will bring you a better standard of living and more personal enjoyment of your free time.

At work you will be relaxed. You will be an excellent leader of your staff – a dependable bunch of people

– maybe family, maybe a partner or friends. You will oversee work of your staff whilst talking to customers, often sitting down with them to enjoy a coffee.

Your supplies will file in and be spirited away by enthusiastic staff whilst customers will congratulate you on your great food, reasonable prices and great service. At the end of the day you will cash up and smile as you count the takings. Your staff will call to you, "Goodbye sir, thank you" as you leave early to let them close up your beloved café. You drive home on top of the world, eagerly awaiting another great day tomorrow.

Well, that's the dream isn't it? I don't expect that many people believe this version of events, but I will tell you in all honesty that some have the perception that this is what life as a café owner will actually be like – and it isn't.

The truth is that running a café is a mixed bag. There are great days and there are days you wish you had never got out of bed. Let's think about that for a moment. Let's think about why you want to run your own café and contrast that with the likely reality.

Introduction

Why you want to run a café	The likely reality
"I want a better lifestyle"	Running a café is a labour-intensive business with low profit margins and often the best performing cafés are those with owners who work long hours. A café can bring you flexibility but you must always remember that when you are not there, there is an additional wage to be accounted for. Owners also have a significant amount of other business duties that aren't restricted to the café's opening hours.
"Money! I want to earn more money!"	Cafés are low margin businesses and can provide a good income if you can get all of the success factors right! You will not become instantly rich.
"I love food / coffee / alcohol and want to work with it; it's my driving passion!"	A passion will keep you going in tough times but running a café is still hard work.
"I can't do anything else and I want to be my own boss"	A café requires great all-round skills. You have to be good at customer service, physically adept, good with finances, able to sort out staff problems, able to do your own marketing, a strong organiser, leader and general all-rounder.

As a café owner you must always be prepared to tackle problems that come up. How would you handle the following scenario?

Breadless

You arrive at the café to find that your bread order isn't there. You call the supplier to find that it was delivered this morning. It's been stolen! Do they have any more? If you have a wonderful bread supplier they may be able to rustle up some more...

This might sound trivial; after all you can buy bread anywhere, can't you? Can you replace your exquisite bread with standard plain bread? Is there a deli near you that has some stock? Do you have time to get in the car and go to the supermarket? Can your staff open the café on their own?

The point I'm trying to make is that being able to handle different problems will help you to be a successful café owner, so before we begin talking about the café you want to buy, we need to check your readiness for the task.

Attributes of a Successful Café Owner

It is critical that you understand what type of person you are in order to understand the way your café will work.

What are your strengths and weaknesses? What do

you like to do? You need to take some time out to be honest with yourself – this is essential to your decision to buy a café, or to buy any business for that matter. The type of person you are will have an enormous impact on both your enjoyment of running a café and your success.

Do you like people?

If you ask a hundred people this question you will probably get 100 "yes" responses. Nobody actually admits that they don't like people – yet I know that there are people who basically do not like dealing with people. The point is that it is a significant advantage if you enjoy dealing with people and can be of detriment to your business if you do not.

A café is a business that relies on regular custom. Daily, weekly, whatever – you will see the same faces time and time again. But how is this regular trade forged? You can serve the best coffee in the world, but if you can't talk to your customers, the likelihood is that they will eventually go to the guy down the road who always smiles and remembers their name.

The fact of the matter is that when you run a café you are dealing with people that you will rely on to turn up day after day. And let's face facts – people can be annoying, difficult, irritating, rude and sometimes downright offensive. If you are the kind of person who can put up with all of that and still smile and say goodbye then it will serve you in good stead.

But if you are more introverted and business-like – don't fret. It isn't impossible to be good at running a café, but you do need to carefully choose the role you perform.

Personally I didn't enjoy working as a waiter, so I quickly adapted myself to become the barista. I chose to recruit staff that were great communicators and great waitstaff, who were adept at building the relationships that would sustain and grow the business.

But I had to adapt. There is simply no running away from contact with the general public. I had to work hard to improve my communication skills. It was a simple choice – if I didn't I would fail.

So if you are a shy person who doesn't like dealing with people, I have to be honest and say owning a café will be challenging. Even if you do not think you are being rude or unfriendly, you may have difficulty building relationships with customers.

> *I know that I fooled myself into thinking that I would be able to build great relationships with all of my customers (and I did with many), but I found that customers can be hard work. It sometimes took me weeks or months to make a connection with a customer but I noticed that staff with the right personality often made the connection quicker.*

Are you efficient and organised?

Are you productive and able to manage your time effectively? Are you organised? Can you make coffee, do rosters, call suppliers, complete order sheets, train staff, design advertising, do your accounts? Can you shift quickly from one task to another?

If you do not consider yourself to be good at organising, your ability to run a café will be tested to the maximum. On a daily basis you will be subjected to a multitude of tasks. You need to have systems, be efficient, be lean. It's not an option – it's a necessity.

Are you good with numbers?

Every week you will add up prices, add up takings, check supplier orders, calculate food costs, pay suppliers, pay staff, update your accounts. Solid financial management is essential. But there are people out there who confess to being "number blind" – so if you are one of them you will need some expertise to guide you.

All of your numbers have to be stored somewhere. Which leads me to my next point.

Are you IT literate?

Even cafés need computers. There are companies that will do things for you, and your accountant will certainly work on your accounts for you, but if you actually want to make money from your business you should try to do the vast majority of the work yourself.

At the very least you will need to provide your accounts in a reasonably legible spreadsheet format. You can pay a bookkeeper to do the basic data entry and get your accountant to do the "hard stuff" but the danger in all of this is that you may lose visibility of your expenses. The benefit of doing it yourself is that it will help you to understand your business better and to keep control of costs.

But computers aren't all about financial management. The better you can use them the greater the benefit for your business: marketing newsletters, special offers, promotions, flyers, advertisements, gift vouchers – you can do all these yourself. And what about the Internet? If you can build a website, use e-mail, understand search engines and social media, this can provide a huge marketing benefit at little or no cost.

Are you physically fit?

Many prospective café owners don't think about being on their feet 14 hours a day. It's tiring; you need to be fit, strong and good with your hands. You have to be confident in your physical ability and you must be honest when looking at your own fitness and physical ability to do it day in, day out.

Can you take the pressure?

The physical aspect is hard, but stress is another matter altogether. Running your own business can be highly stressful. If the café is quiet you may worry about going broke, if you are busy you may worry about service slipping! But different people are able to handle it better than others. If you are the kind of person who can smile when things aren't at their best you will have an advantage. It will help you to steer the ship on a steady course and you will enjoy running the café all the more for it.

> *One of my former baristas was a forty-five year old stockbroker who bought his own café. 12 months later he was being carried out of the café on a stretcher with a suspected heart attack.*

How do you like to work?

You need to think hard about the role that you will perform in the café as this will be closely linked to the kind of person you are and also your levels of trust. There are advantages and disadvantages of each type of role (which we will discuss later), and there is nothing to say that you can't be a chef / waiter / kitchen-hand / barista if you want to be, but the chances are that you will tend to naturally fall into the role you can do best or enjoy best.

Café Roles

Let's have a look at some of the typical roles in a café and some of the key attributes.

Role	Attributes required	Advantages of owner performing role	Disadvantages of owner performing role
Cashier	Good interpersonal skills, Trustworthy	Keep tight control of cash, build relationships with customers	Not many cafés can afford to have a cashier role as a full time position.
Barista	Dexterity, Fitness	Ensure high quality coffee, able to monitor floor staff and cash register	Making coffee is a full-time role and there is little time to do other café tasks. Hard to control quality of food output.
Waitstaff	Fitness, ability to multi-task, outgoing personality	Build relationships with customers, ensure quality service / food output	Difficult to control till / coffee quality.
Chef	Ability to multi-task, planning skills, culinary skills	Highest cost role so saves greatest amount of money	Difficult to oversee floor service / quality of coffee / cash register.
Kitchen-hand	Fitness	Visibility of food standards	No visibility of coffee / till / floor service. Physical, dirty job.

By now you should have a rough idea of where you might fit in to a café, but whatever role (or multiple roles) you choose to perform the chances are that at some stage you will be required to do all of them. Make sure you learn each role and become proficient at all of them.

So we've talked about the attributes required to be a café owner, so let's turn our attention to the café industry and try to dispel a few myths about small business.

Fear of Failure

At any one time, there are hundreds of cafés for sale in Australian capital cities. The majority of cafés are for sale by people who were not able to successfully get the returns they anticipated. By you reading this book, you are doing your homework so that you are better informed than those other owners.

Despite claims to the contrary, the statistics on café failure are positive for café owners.

In *"Business Failure and Change: An Australian Perspective" (2000)* the Productivity Commission indicate that:

- **Two-thirds of businesses are still operating after five years and almost one-half are still operating after ten years**

- **Only 7.5% of businesses exit each year**
- **Less than 0.5% of businesses exit each year due to 'catastrophic' failure e.g. going bankrupt**
- **Exit rates are higher for businesses less than 2 years old**

Whatever the statistics say, nothing will ever take the place of your own research – by this I mean getting your *own* statistics – and I'll talk about this later.

But all in all, the message is "don't believe the hype". The statistics show that owning a café isn't as risky as it is made out to be.

Before You Start Looking For A Café

So, after all that you've read you're still keen? Great – now you need to do some thorough groundwork.

Can You Buy a Café?

There are many café options available to you and it's a very personal decision as to what type of café you will buy. I would strongly encourage you to trust your instincts on this one. There is a simple logic: if you buy a café that you personally like, you will be more in-tune with your customers and their expectations.

It is important that you can relate to your customers and drive the business in the right direction. Whilst small changes in direction can improve a business, radical changes in direction and misjudging your customer base can prove to be disastrous. An extreme example: if you run a café that has an older clientele and you decide that you are going to change the menu to burgers and fries and play loud music, it is highly unlikely that your current customer base are going to stick around. Pick a market that you can relate to and build upon with your knowledge.

So before you jump headlong into the purchasing process, ask yourself some hard questions:

How Much Do I Want to Spend?

Some might say it's not so much a case of "How much do I *want* to spend?" as a case of "How much do I *have* to spend?" There is some truth in this, depending on where your money is coming from. If you have a stack of cash to spend and don't need to borrow to finance the purchase I would say the question is "How much do I want to spend?" The reason for this is that it may not be prudent to splash all your cash on the biggest and best. If you buy a large and very busy café, it could prove to be overwhelming (and you have a lot more to lose financially).

Now if you are financing the purchase the question is more likely to be "How much do I have to spend?" To be able to borrow to purchase you will need a deposit (or equity) which will determine the amount you can borrow. e.g. If you have $50k you may be able to borrow $250k, but again, do you want a small or large café? If you are borrowing to finance, the loan will be based upon the financials of the business and the security you can provide the lender (although it may be slightly easier to borrow if you intend to purchase a franchise). The point is that you need to think about the amount you are going to borrow and decide if you feel comfortable with that amount. Although you are investing in a business, if things go wrong you will still have the loan to pay.

Do I Want Something Big or Small?

Some people just like to feel big and important – that's OK! Some people like a little café that is more manageable but which won't make them a fortune (generally). It is entirely up to you, so think about what you would prefer – something big with lots of staff, something small with a few staff or maybe something in-between. The size of café will have many other implications which we will discuss later on, but it's important that you go for a size that will match your skills and aspirations for the business.

> *If you have never run a café before, I always suggest that people begin with a smaller café then either expand the number of cafés gradually or buy a bigger / busier café when they feel able to handle it.*

Do I want a Franchise or an "Independent" Café?

A franchised café is a café concept that is owned by a company and sold as a reproducible commodity business. You might think of it as the replication of a café concept. The franchisor sells a café as a business to the franchisee who in turn agrees to run the café according to the guidelines and procedures of the franchisor. The franchisor provides backing to the franchisee in terms of people, procedures, systems, marketing, etc. – basically everything required to run the business. In return the franchisee usually agrees to pay both initial (one-off) and ongoing franchise fees – typically a percentage of turnover.

Many new café owners start off with franchises as they are viewed as a "safe bet" – this is far from the truth. Let's look at some of the major differences of a franchised café:

Price	Café franchises will be typically 2-3 times more expensive than an independent café.
Operation	Café franchises are generally easier to operate than independent cafés due to the structured processes and procedures in place – however, franchisees have to run the business as dictated by the franchisor.
Marketing	All marketing is controlled via head office and franchisees have little say in the marketing activities undertaken.
Suppliers	Franchised cafés are typically tied to buying their products from the franchisor (although some variation is usually allowed).
Start-up	The franchisor is fully involved with the start-up process for new cafés, including location selection, fit-out and promotions.
Location	Typically franchises are "mass market" offerings and are therefore best suited to high traffic areas such as shopping malls. This typically means that lease payments will be high and that the café has to operate at "high volume" levels to survive.

For some people a café franchise is an ideal first step as they are generally easier to run and the franchisor offers continual support for the franchisee. Saying that, there are also poorly run "flash in the pan" franchises out there that seek to take advantage of the unwary. Whether you decide to buy a franchise or an independent café, both require thorough due diligence.

What Sort of Café Would I Enjoy Working In?

What I am trying to say here is to be honest with yourself and go for something that appeals to you. You will have to work in the place so you'd better like it! Also think about the kind of work you are likely to perform. For example, if you buy a full food café (i.e. with a chef and "proper" food) there is a big difference between that and a café offering soup, sandwiches and re-heated food.

Also, it's important to think about the style of café that you want to own. If you want a cool, trendy café then buy a cool, trendy café. Don't try to turn a sow's ear into a silk purse. It isn't impossible to do well buying a place and changing it to suit a new demographic, but if you haven't owned your own café before you will have additional challenges that may be overwhelming. In short, don't do it unless you have some great support or someone with experience to help you along the way.

What Location Would I Prefer?

Think carefully about where you buy your café and what you consider to be an acceptable commuting distance. Also bear in mind that it is more than likely that you will need to be able to drive. A car or van is a necessity in the café game, so take into account any potential commuting / traffic time by car.

> *Is a car or van essential for a café owner? Yes! You will need a practical car for a variety of reasons – carrying stock, equipment and maybe even the day's laundry.*

Overall, the best strategy is to keep an open mind and to go and look at a lot of different cafés that are for sale. You'll quickly decide what you do and don't like. Now, hardcore business types will be screaming at me here because it sounds like I am telling you to buy a café based on whether you think it looks good. This is not the case. A good purchase depends upon ticking all the right boxes – one of those is finding something that suits you and that you feel you can be happy working within. Don't forget that a huge part of running a business is about making money. I'll discuss the financial side of things further on in this chapter.

But for now, it is important to get out and look, look, look. It's a bit like buying a house – you will feel if a business is right or wrong in the pit of your stomach – but with the added complexity of having to assess the business (both financially or otherwise). It is crucially important to separate head and heart. Don't be blinded by falling in love with a business. By all means go for something that suits you, but if it doesn't tick all the boxes then be prepared to let it go.

The Café Buying Process

The diagram on the following page gives a high level overview of the process of buying a café. As we proceed we will discuss each stage of the process in detail.

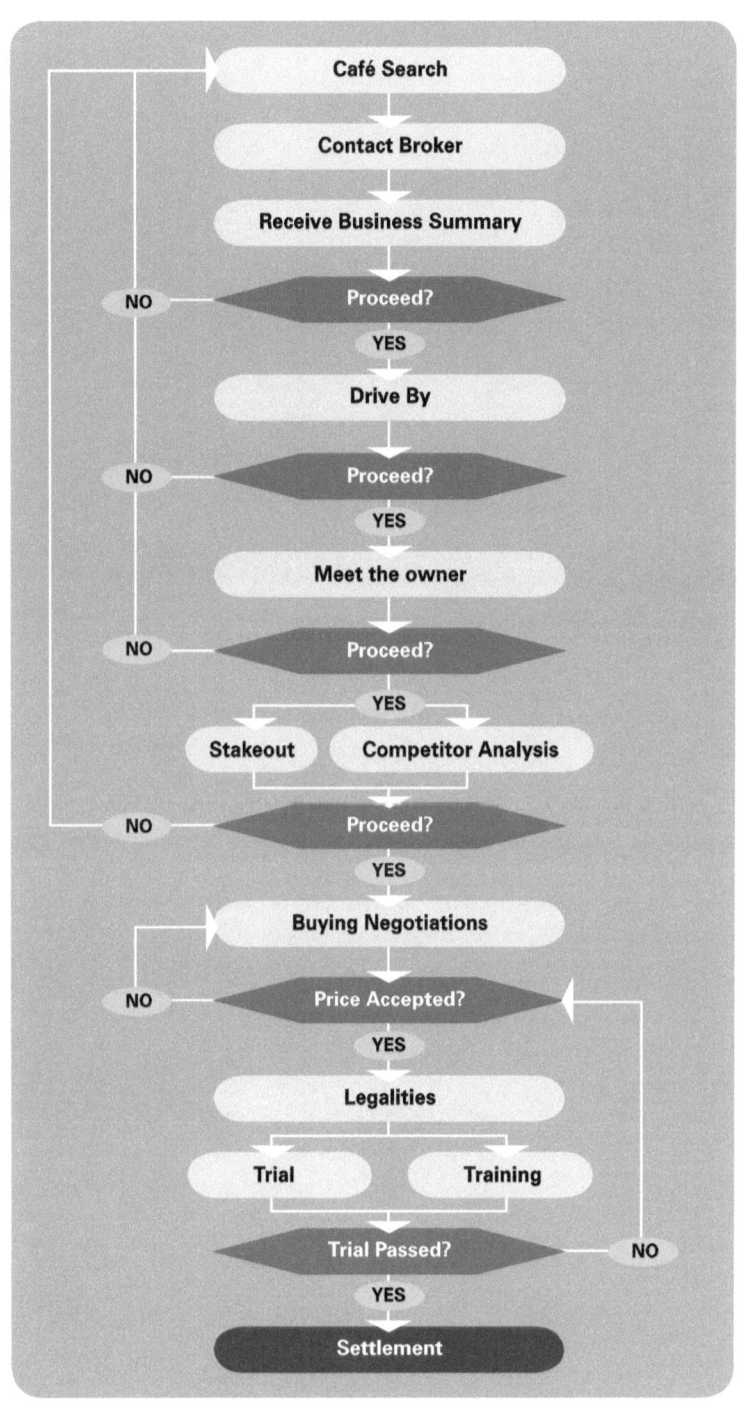

Finding A Café To Buy

The two people you need to make contact with are an accountant and a solicitor. If you really want to dot all the "i's" and cross all the "t's" you might want to consider having a hospitality consultant fully assess the café. You wouldn't buy a house without a survey so don't buy a café without a thorough analysis.

Referral can often be a good way to find an accountant or solicitor but make sure you ask the referrer what makes the person a good choice. The referrer may have very different opinions on what they look for and may also have very different business interests which lead to very different needs.

It is important to get these people in place and ready to go as the buying process can often be surprisingly competitive. For example, you may find a café that you want to buy but there is a lot of interest in it. If you have your solicitor and accountant ready to go you have the opportunity to get ahead of those that are not as organised as you are. It can make the difference between getting the café of your dreams or missing out.

The Accountant

Why you need to find a good accountant:

- They can assist with your business plan

- They will help you to set up an appropriate company structure (which helps to get the most out of the tax system)

- They will help you to set up your accounting systems

- They will advise you on the financial aspects of the business purchase

- They will ensure that you submit all your required tax documentation on time.

But getting a good accountant can be tricky. There are lots out there and they aren't cheap! So what should you expect from an accountant?

- They will provide an initial consultation free of charge

- They will come to you – you're busy running your business so make sure that they are willing to come to you (you are the client!)

- They will provide templates (e.g. Excel spreadsheets) or provide assistance on setting up your financial systems

- They will provide a fixed price for your annual tax return
- They include general enquiries (throughout the year) as "part of the deal"
- They have a set hourly rate for other work i.e. work that isn't "general enquiries".

The Solicitor

Why you need a good solicitor...
- To explain the buying process – including deposits, trial periods, etc.
- To understand the fine print in contracts e.g. the lease
- To warn you of any legal pitfalls
- To complete the deal!

What makes a good solicitor?
- They aren't too busy to see you when you really need them
- They understand the legalities of cafés and small business
- They understand the legal requirements of councils
- They have experience with leases and property.

Once you have your support network in place, you are ready to really hit the road and begin your search.

Finding a Café

Generally the best place to start looking is in the major newspapers and online. But if you have the time, check both as there are exceptions that are only advertised in one or the other. Sometimes newsagencies have magazines which list businesses for sale.

Most businesses are sold via business brokers. You will find that most café advertisements will have the name of the business broker on it. However, you will also find that some are for sale independently. Like buying a house directly from the owner, this can be a tricky and awkward process. It is best in this scenario to employ the services of a buying agent to handle the negotiations.

Contacting the Broker

It is definitely worth your while to have a look in the newspaper or online and identify who the major business brokers are in your area and to contact them directly to let them know what you are looking for. It is important to give them a clear brief about what you are looking for – a lot of time can be wasted with them showing you businesses that are wrong if you aren't clear.

The role of a business broker is to represent the vendor, so it still falls to you to ask as many relevant questions as you need, and to assess how well the answers satisfy you. Many café buyers make the mistake of believing the information that the broker provides is accurate, and often it is far from it.

Personal Approach

If you see a café that you like you can also approach the owner directly to see if they are willing to sell it to you. All businesses are for sale at the right price – but be aware that you will undoubtedly pay a premium for the business. If you take this approach it is important to have the financials of the business thoroughly assessed by both an accountant and licenced valuer.

Analysing The Business Summary

When you inquire about cafés that you are interested in, you will be asked by the broker or seller to complete a non-disclosure agreement. This is a legal document that basically is designed to make sure that you don't go and tell others about the details of the business (if you did they could take legal action against you). A non-disclosure agreement (or NDA as it's commonly known) is standard practice and isn't anything you need to overly concern yourself with. Just sign the forms and send them back. No NDA equals no information, so it's not as if you have any choice.

After you have sent the NDA back, the broker will send you what they call a business summary. This is a 1 or 2 page document that gives you a high level overview of the café. It will usually contain details such as:

- Description of the café
- Location
- Hours of operation
- Reason for sale
- Equipment
- Staff
- Financials.

An Example of a Business Summary

Café Mocha, 62 Pleasant Street, Pleasantville (nearest cross-street Nice Street)	
Classification	Café
Trading Hours	6 Days Tuesday-Friday 7.30am-5pm Saturday-Sunday 8am-5pm
Parking	1-2 parking spaces
Established	January 1999
Trial	Negotiable
Equipment	All in good working order
Premises	Fronts onto Pleasant Street
Delivery Access	Front
Size	Approx 80m²
Seating Capacity	22 Indoor, 18 Outdoor
Grease Trap	Yes
Reason for Sale	Other business interests
Nature of Business	Typical café selling salads, sandwiches, pastas, risottos and all day breakfast
Nature of Surrounding businesses	Typical retail: Opposite street Chinese takeaway, locksmith, TAB, florist, bakery
	Businesses: Pleasantville Hotel adjacent

Analysing The Business Summary

Owner's Role	Owner is hands-on, ordering stock, serving customers, making coffee
Breakup of TYPICAL WEEKLY PURCHASES:	Sales/Purchases: Bread $230, Cakes $100, Dry Goods $170, Fish & Seafood $60, Fruit & Vegetables $160, Meat $200, Poultry $75, Smallgoods and Deli Items $60, Other $130, Coffee $230, Milk $210, Mineral Water $30, Soft Drinks $60, Other $45
Business Potential	Extend hours e.g. open Mondays and open as a restaurant in the evenings. Mediterranean style at present, but any style cuisine could be offered
Comments	• Two dry stores available, use of Gym and Spas and Sauna • No opposition in close proximity • This café has an excellent finish, commercial kitchen and a stainless steel finish. Facing north to capture morning sun and has an outside terrace for smokers • 10-12kgs of coffee a week. Crema Bella blend. • A three-month bank guarantee is required. • Voted in top ten breakfast cafés by Hungry magazine
Term Of Lease	5 x 5
Commencement Date	On negotiation

Increases / Reviews	4% plus outgoings Strata Levy $1,532pa, Council Rates $1,564pa, Water rates $373pq 3-month Bank Guarantee
Staff	Full-time Owner(s) 1, Casual Owner(s) 1, Full-time Staff 1, Casual Staff 5
Asking Price	$120,000
Stock	$2,000
Financial Projections	Based on a weekly Turnover of $7,700 Sales (Including GST)
TOTAL INCOME	$7,700
Operating Expenses (Including GST)	Outgoings $88, Rent $924 TOTAL OPERATING EXPENSES $1,012
Net Profit	$140,000pa

At first glance you look at the business's profit and you think "Fantastic, it's making $140k per year and it only costs $120k!" but let's look into that in a bit more detail…

Reliability of the Business Summary

It is critically important for you to understand that the business summary is not the truth. It may be a version of the truth, but the details within the business summary need to be thoroughly scrutinised. Do not, under any circumstances, make a business purchase decision based solely on the information provided in the business summary.

There are several reasons for this:

- It is written by the broker who is pitching the business in its best light
- Figures are often altered to represent future scenarios
- Assumptions are made about staffing
- Accuracy of information cannot be guaranteed
- It does not take into account your own circumstances.

However, prior to meeting the owner it is advisable to obtain detailed certified accounts and to analyse these thoroughly…

Financials

When you ask the broker to see the accounts, he will point you towards the Business Summary. It is better that you ask to see the "certified accounts", since these represent a much more accurate view of the business financials.

Try to obtain as many sets of accounts as you possibly can. It is a legal requirement to produce company accounts for tax purposes on a yearly basis, so if the café has been, for example, in operation for 6 years there should be 6 years of accounts. The more financial information you can obtain the better – particularly if you can get financial information over a period of years, as this can help you to identify trends. For example, sales increasing or decreasing, costs rising, etc. It can help to show you what direction the business has been heading in. But even with certified accounts there can be a great deal of smoke and mirrors…

How to Read the Financials

The following sections will help you to look at the figures, understand what they mean and to find out how the business is really performing.

The most critical figure in all of this is **net profit.** The way to think of the financials is quite simple: turnover – costs = net profit. But remember that brokers will make assumptions to make a business look more attractive than it actually is. For example, you may find an assumption in the business summary in the fine print at the end such as, "Business currently being run under management but net profit based on business being run by two owners". They then make the assumption that two owners would work 60 hours a week each and pay themselves $50k a year each. What? That equates to an extra $100k profit plus the $40k profit they say it's already making – so the business is making a total profit of $140k a year – wow! So when you cast your eyes over the business summary you see $140k a year profit and jump eagerly to grab your chequebook. You will find that in almost every circumstance the café isn't making anything like the money claimed by the broker in the scenario described.

The only truly reliable way to really see how much money it is making is to look at the accounts.

The Percentage Guide

The percentage guide is a methodology that café owners use to manage the costs of their business. It states that each cost should fall into a category which makes up a particular percentage of turnover (ex GST), as follows:

Category	%
Staff Wages	25-35
Food	25-35
Rent	10-15
Other (utilities, insurance, repairs etc)	10-20
Profit	Whatever is left!

The percentage guide is useful, but the most important thing to remember is that there must be balance. For example, if the staff costs are high, this should be balanced by the food costs or rent being a bit lower. You can see that if all your costs are at the top end (35+35+15+20=105%) – you will be losing money!!! However, if you can keep all of your costs low (25+25+10+10) you will make a 30% profit (which is very good for a café). What you should do when looking at the financials is to work out the percentage for each item.

We will discuss some of the flaws of the percentage method later when we consider pricing and the menu, but for now use it as a guide (but never a rule). Again, remember that net profit is king – or as they say *"Turnover is vanity, profit is sanity"*.

Turnover

Turnover is simply the $ amount of sales the business

makes in a year. Don't be blinded by impressive turnover figures (remember "turnover is vanity"!). Also ensure that you find out how many weeks a year the café is open and divide the total turnover by the amount of weeks to get the weekly average. Once you have the weekly average, divide this by the number of days the café is open. There is a big difference in profitability between a café turning over $10k a week and being open 5 days a week than one turning over $10k a week and being open 7 days.

> *Tip: if you want to compare a café trading 5 days as against one trading 7, take the turnover for the café that is open 7 days, divide it by 7 and multiply by 5. It may also help you compare different cafés if you divide the weekly turnover by the number of hours the business is open: e.g.*
>
> *60 hours per week at $10,000pw turnover = $167 per hour*
>
> *80 hours per week at $10,000pw turnover = $125 per hour*

Keeping the café open for 80 hours per week will, obviously, cost more than opening for 60 hours per week – in terms of extra electricity, gas, labour etc.

Turnover may or may not be displayed as including GST. Be careful with this. If turnover includes GST you need to take 10% off the turnover figure provided (tip - divide the turnover by 11 to find the GST amount). Do not consider GST in turnover to be yours.

In a café, approximately 80% of the GST (included in turnover) will need to be paid to the government. This is because there aren't many expenses within a café that are subject to GST (the main exception being rent).

The Cash Dilemma

One of the biggest problems you may encounter with buying a café is undeclared turnover, or in other words "cash sales".

Some cafés will (illegally) take cash and not declare it as taxable "turnover" i.e. they put it "in their pocket" rather than putting it through the till and therefore avoid paying the 10% GST on it. They also frequently use the cash to pay staff who (for one reason or another) want to avoid any record of themselves receiving income from the café.

So what do you do when you look at a café for sale and they tell you that "on paper" they take $7,000 per week but in reality they take in $10,000 – with $3,000 of that as "cash"?

Ultimately there is no foolproof way of knowing exactly how much they are taking, but we can estimate

Analysing The Business Summary

by using our percentage method. This states that the average *cost of goods* will be 30%. For example, if the sales are reported to be $10,000 per week, the cost of goods should be approximately $3,000 per week.

Ask the vendor for 3-6 month's worth of their receipts for cost of goods, i.e. food purchases, etc. These receipts should then be totalled and divided by the number of weeks during that period. e.g. 6 months = 26 weeks:

Turnover (Total)	$10,000
Turnover (On paper)	$7,000
Turnover (Cash)	$3,000
Cost of Goods (6 Months)	$77,532
Number of Weeks	26
Cost of Goods Per Week	$2,982
Estimated Turnover	$9,940

Note: to calculate estimated weekly turnover, divide the weekly COG figure by three then multiply this by 10.

If the vendor refuses to provide you with the receipts for cost of goods then you should take only the "on paper" turnover as the basis of your analysis. To do anything other than this would be to submit yourself to an unacceptable level of risk.

Gross Profit

Gross profit is turnover minus the cost of goods. It is useful to know the Gross Profit Margin as a guide to business performance. Gross Margin = Sales (100%) less the Cost of Goods. A Gross Margin of 70% is considered to be the industry average. A Gross Margin of 60% reflects that the business is inefficient or wasteful.

Cost of Goods

Cost of goods is the materials cost required to produce your output. Essentially, cost of goods is your food cost, but it will also include all items required to produce your service, such as napkins, etc.

Food Cost

Food cost, as stated before, should be approximately 25-35% of sales, but this will vary according to the type of café. For example, if you are selling lots of seafood your % cost may be more towards the 35% mark. If you are selling just toast and soup it might be down at 20%. Take the total food cost $ amount and divide this by the turnover amount to get the percentage. You will need to know your costs as a guide to your menu pricing policy. High cost seafood should command a higher price. This will push down the food cost percentage of sales.

e.g. Food Cost $2,000 per Week, Turnover $6,000 per week = 33% Cost of Goods.

Food cost is the cost of the food items required to produce your menu items. It is important to note that fresh foods do not include GST. However, foods such as cakes that are pre-prepared do include GST. (Don't worry about that too much just now as we will explore the world of GST later in the section on Business Activity Statements.)

Food cost is obviously a very important part of assessing a café because it is likely to be one of your largest expenses, and it is one that should be tightly controlled.

Labour / Staff

Labour is the cost of your staff. Other staff expenses can sometimes be hidden under other categories, such as "Contractors" or "Consultants". Labour also may or may not include the owner's wages. It is important to identify where the owner's wages are in the financials.

Labour costs, along with food costs are likely to be your biggest expense. Expect to have staff costs between 25-35%. Many cafés choose to pay staff in cash, i.e. not "on the books". This is a hidden cost that can distort the true picture of how the business is running. Don't be afraid to ask the owner which staff are paid cash – but they may not always give you an honest answer. Remember, paying staff "off the books" with cash is illegal.

Roster vs. Staff Costs

A key way to find out about staffing is to obtain a weekly roster. This roster should contain all staff working over a seven-day period and should be broken down to an hourly level if possible.

Ideally it should include:

- Staff names
- Staff roles e.g. team leader / supervisor / chef / waitress, etc.
- Pay rate
- Total hours worked by each staff member
- Total $ staff cost per day
- Total $ staff cost per week.

A good broker will give you a roster in this format. Chances are the roster will be skewed towards indicating a lower staff level, so make several visits to the cafés and observe the number and type of staff.

Analysing the Roster

To analyse the roster the first thing you should do is to look at the wage costs in the financials and divide this by the number of weeks the café is open during the year. Next, compare this to the total weekly staff costs in the roster.

The costs will not be identical (as the roster will usually be for a "typical" week) but they should be very similar. If not, alarm bells should be ringing and you should be asking the broker to provide details of why there is a discrepancy. Any discrepancy is a cause for concern and requires more detailed analysis. It could simply be that the owner is a disorganised person.

Fixed & Variable Costs

Fixed costs are costs to the business that tend to remain the same or "fixed" over a period of time. For example, the most common fixed cost is rent. Rent will be agreed at a set rate, usually on a yearly basis with a percentage increase per year.

Other fixed costs are likely to include:

- Council rates
- Strata rates
- Rental costs for equipment, etc.

Fixed costs are important to consider as they are independent of turnover, i.e. no matter how much – or how little – the business is taking in, you still have to pay them.

All other costs are known as **variable costs,** and they will tend to vary in direct relation to turnover. This makes sense when you consider that if you get busier you will need to buy more food to meet demand and more staff to serve more customers. The opposite is also true – less custom and you will need less food and less staff.

If you are managing the business properly, your café's variable costs will drop if the turnover starts to drop – however the fixed costs will remain and these will start to represent a bigger percentage of your overall costs. This is where a business can get into trouble. So the bottom line is that fixed costs need to be looked at carefully to ensure they will not represent too much of a burden if times get tough.

On the contrary, as turnover increases, profitability can increase by a proportionately larger amount, as the following example shows:

Turnover	$6,000	$7,000	$8,000
Variable Costs (50%)	$3,000	$3,500	$4,000
Fixed Costs	$2,500	$2,500	$2,500
Weekly Profit	$500	$1,000	$1,500

If you bought the café with a turnover of $6,000 and profits of $500 (8%) and you can increase the turnover to $7,000, the profit margin increases to $1,000 (14%). At a turnover of $8,000 the profit margin increases to $1,500 (19%).

The profit margin has more than doubled even though turnover has only increased by one third. The limit on your growth is simply the capacity of the café. If you can outgrow the capacity, it is time to find a bigger, better café or, perhaps, to open a second one.

Rent

Rent is a critical (fixed) cost and should represent 10-15% of turnover. Rent is subject to GST so be careful to check whether the rent stated in the business summary includes or excludes GST.

Rent will usually be based on a lease which runs for a certain period of time. Depending on the café you may purchase an existing lease e.g. one that was initiated by someone else and which has some time to run. Usually leases have an inbuilt yearly percentage increase. This might be a fixed amount, e.g. 4% or CPI (Consumer Price Index – a percentage amount measured by government authorities based on the average cost increases of a range of products). It is important to consider the impact that this percentage increase will have on future years, particularly if the rent is high at the time of purchase. A useful exercise is to calculate the percentage of total turnover that rent represents if turnover stays constant over a number of years.

Let's now return to the business summary example and put into practice some of the information just learned.

Analysing The Business Summary - An Example

Café name: Café Mocha

Consider the name. Unless the name is truly awful, try not to change it. If you do decide to change it remember that you will have to spend money on new signage, stationery, websites, etc. You will also lose any equity in the name, e.g. if the café has had positive reviews and good PR in the past. If you do decide to change it, try to come up with something that encapsulates the entire business, not something bland and uninspiring like "Fred's Café".

Location: 62 Pleasant Street, Pleasantville. (Nearest cross-street, Nice Street)

Go to the location, look at the amount of passing trade and the position. Is it busy? Is it pleasant? Attractive? Is it a main road? Can customers park easily?

Classification: Café

Double check that the business has consent to operate as a café. Contact the local council to make sure everything is in place, or ask your solicitor to do this for you.

Trading Hours: 6 Days
Tue-Fri: 7.30 a.m. - 5 p.m., Sat-Sun: 8 a.m. - 5 p.m.

Calculate the total hours that the business is open. In this case it is 38 during the week and 18 on the weekend. Total hours open = 56. However, bear in mind that this does not include time spent opening and closing (approx 2 hours per day x 6 days = 12 hours). So in total the weekly hours will be approximately 68 hours a week. As an owner you may have to work these 68 hours.

Most cafés restrict their operation to morning and lunchtime trade, but there are quite a few that also open at night. If you are looking at buying a café that is open at night think about the level of commitment that this will require. How will you manage the staffing? What days and hours will you work? Will you close after lunch and re-open for dinner or stay open? When will you make time to prepare for evening trade? Try not to over commit yourself.

Parking: 1-2 parking spaces

Here you should clarify what 1-2 spaces means! Is it one space or two? In this instance it turned out to be one large car parking space that could fit two cars. Parking is important as you will need a car. Often you will be carrying things in and out of your car. Even if you decide to have stock delivered there are always things that you need to carry back and forth from home, e.g. cloths and uniforms to be washed.

Established: January 1999

The establishment date is good to know – the longer the business has been established, the less chance there is of it failing. It also gives you an exact understanding of how many years' accounts you can ask for – although it is unlikely that any business will give you accounts further back than about 3 years. However, they may do this to show you how well the business did a few years further back, e.g. under a different owner.

Although it is an Australian taxation requirement that financial records be kept for 7 years, there is no law that states that the café owner has to show these records to you.

In this example the business has been in operation for almost 13 years so there should be at least 7 full years of accounts available – however, if you can get the last three years' complete accounts, this is acceptable.

Trial: Negotiable

The trial period is a set period, e.g. 1 week that gives you an opportunity to view the business on a daily basis and to confirm the turnover as specified in the business summary. The trial period takes place after you have agreed a price to buy the business, but before the settlement has taken place. We will discuss the trial process in more detail later.

Equipment: All in good working order

Equipment generally will cover kitchen equipment such as ovens, deep fat fryers, blenders, pots and pans, etc. Ensure that you ask for a list of all the equipment and confirm that all equipment on the list is in full operation: "good working order" may mean that it works, even though it is 30 years old and stuck together with sticky tape.

The following list details some of the key items of equipment that you will require. Not all cafés will require everything on this list, but it would be very surprising if they didn't have them. If there is equipment missing you should ask them how they get by without it.

Something that is important to know is that you are buying a certain amount of capital in the equipment. That is if a business (such as this one) is valued at $120k then a good proportion of that (e.g. $30-40k) will be made up of the value of the equipment. The rest is "goodwill" to account for the custom you are buying.

The greater the value placed upon equipment the greater the depreciable amount for tax purposes. Saying that, goodwill is the biggest determinant of the value of the business. A café isn't worth much without goodwill, never mind how good the equipment is.

Note: All equipment should be commercial quality equipment – appliances designed for home use will neither last or will have the capacity for café use.

Equipment Checklist

When you visit the café, use the following checklist to note what equipment is present and what condition it is in. Check your notes against the equipment details in the business summary.

Equipment	Present	Condition
Oven		
Stove		
Grill		
Commercial Toaster		
Dishwasher		
Ice machine		
Refrigeration		
Freezer		
Deep Fryer		
Blender		
Food processor		
Milkshake maker		
Coffee machine		
Coffee grinder		
Stereo system		
Pots & pans		
Spoons, ladles, etc.		
Crockery & cutlery		
Plastic containers / Tupperware		

Premises: Fronts onto Pleasant Street

Again, check the aspect of the street, parking, etc.

Delivery Access: Front

Access is important as this will designate where your deliveries come in. In this case access is from the front, which is not ideal; suppliers will have to come through the front of the café with their deliveries. This is not particularly pleasant from a customer point of view. Rear access is better as your customers will not have to put up with clunking trolleys, sweaty delivery men and large amounts of boxes stacked in the café.

Size: Approximately 80m²

There isn't much you can do with the size, but you should bear the size in mind if you are thinking about altering the layout of the café in any way. The size will dictate the size of kitchen and amount of internal seating you can have (which will in turn dictate the type of food you can serve and the amount of money you can turn over per hour).

Seating Capacity: 22 Indoor, 18 Outdoor

The seating capacity will ultimately limit your capacity to make money so is a very important number. In this case the café has 40 seats – small, but not tiny. It is useful to look at the average customer spend (you can ask the owner for this) and multiply this by the seating capacity. Using the assumption that the average customer will spend an hour in the café, the number of seats x average $ spend will give the *turnover ceiling* per hour. For example, say this café has an average spend of $20 per person, it will have a *maximum* hourly turnover of $800. However, cafés usually operate far from capacity. The turnover ceiling is critically important in peak periods when the café can reach capacity.

> *A newly opened café had a problem – they were packed! Why was this a problem? On weekends they were full at peak periods – so much so that they had to turn customers away. The reason? – they only had 20 seats. They were very popular but their turnover ceiling was extremely low due to their limited seating capacity. The business proved to be unsustainable and they closed within a year of opening.*

Grease Trap: Yes

A grease trap is basically a large pit in the ground where all the cooking fat and waste from your grills is stored. Having a grease trap makes it significantly easier to be able to manage the "heavy cooking" – otherwise you may be limited to selling lighter foods that have less grease run-off such as sandwiches and pre-prepared foods. In other words, if you want to run a café with a full range of food, it is of great benefit to have a grease trap.

If you buy a café you should ask for plans of the café clearly showing where the grease trap is and the access required to empty it.

Note: A grease trap needs to be emptied approximately every 6 months and this will cost several hundred dollars. There are a number of companies that provide this service. The smell of a grease trap being emptied is highly unpleasant. If the grease trap is located near to your customer areas it is best if it is emptied outside of business hours.

Reason for Sale: Other business interests

You are often unlikely to get an honest answer as to why someone is selling a café but it does happen. After all, people do retire and people do build up businesses with the aim of making a profit selling them. However, the stated reasons for sale may disguise the true reasons for the sale. You will never find a reason for sale such as, "We're not making any money" or "A franchise is about to open next door and take all my custom". The reason you are likely to be given is typically a vague, non-descript statement. But you should ask the question anyway, ask them what their "other business interests" are – and if what they say sounds unrealistic or vague, you know that they are hiding the true reason for the sale, which may not be a good sign.

Ultimately be cautious and try to get as much information on the reason for sale when you meet the owner.

Nature of Business: Typical café selling salads, sandwiches, pastas, risottos and all day breakfast

This information won't provide any particularly great insights into the business. You will be able to confirm the accuracy of this information simply by visiting the café and looking at the menu. We will discuss analysing the menu later on.

Nature of surrounding area: Typical retail. Opposite street – Chinese takeaway, locksmith, TAB, florist, bakery, Pleasantville Hotel adjacent

The surrounding businesses are also vitally important. Local businesses have customers that might also frequent your café. Local businesses represent a great potential market for loyal local customers, i.e. staff working there. Look at the local businesses and ask how much footfall they might be able to generate – particularly big draw-cards like supermarkets or other large retail outlets that attract large amounts of customers. Look overhead for professional offices – accountants, solicitors, dentists, etc.

Owners Role: Owner is hands-on, ordering stock, serving customers, making coffee

Although you may have your own ideas about the type of work you would like to do in the café, a description of the owner's role may help to identify what you are likely to have to do. For example, in a café of this size, if you want to just take the cash and order stock you are going to have to pay someone to fill in all the duties you don't want to do. In this example you will need to pay a barista approximately $40k a year. You can take that $40k off your yearly profit and stand around chatting to customers or you can work hard and put it in your pocket.

Breakup of typical weekly purchases: Bread $230, Cakes $100, Dry Goods $170, Fish & Seafood $60, Fruit & Vegetables $160, Meat $200, Poultry $75, Smallgoods and Deli Items $60, Other $130, Coffee $230, Milk $210, Mineral Water $30, Soft Drinks $60, Other $45

The total of this is $1,760. That represents 25% of turnover (turnover excluding GST). This is a good percentage according to our percentage guide. You can double check this total by looking at the percentage cost of goods, which comes in at about 24%. So it is likely that these figures are fairly accurate. But if you want to be absolutely sure ask the owner for a sample of invoices from their suppliers. Ideally ask for all invoices for 6 months – add them up and divide by the number of weeks to see if it matches the percentage you originally calculated. You will also need to match the cost of goods to the sales figures for the same period in time to be able to perform the calculation. Another thing to question in this example is the two "other" categories.

Business Potential: Extend hours e.g. open Mondays and open as a restaurant in the evenings. Mediterranean style at present, but any style cuisine could be offered

While some of this may be true, remember this is a sales tactic designed to make you excited about the business. In this example the actual café was located in a suburb that was quiet at night and upon further examination of council documents was found to be only able to open until 9pm. So unless changes were made via council (which could be a long and costly process) the café was not able to open in the evenings. The statement about being able to change to any cuisine is somewhat redundant – it is usually quite easy to change to any other type of cuisine.

Other Comments:
- ***Two dry stores available, use of Gym and Spas and Sauna***

- **No opposition in close proximity**
- **This café has an excellent finish, a commercial kitchen and a stainless steel finish**
- **Facing north to capture morning sun and has an outside terrace for smokers**
- **10-12kgs of coffee a week. Crema Bella blend**
- **A three-month bank guarantee is required**
- **Voted in top ten breakfast cafés by Hungry magazine.**

Let's look at those one by one…

- **Two dry stores available, use of Gym and Spas and Sauna**

Drystores are where you store your goods that aren't perishable. All cafés need a drystore, and the bigger you can get the better, as you can use them for a multitude of things, e.g. change room for when you accidentally pour a jug of soy milk all over yourself. However, size can vary and what is a drystore to one person is a cupboard to another.

Don't worry about the use of spas and sauna – the last thing you will feel like at the end of the day is a session at the gym. A nice sauna at the end of the day sounds like a nice way to unwind but by the time you close up all sweaty and smelling of garbage all you will be interested in is dinner, a glass of wine and bed!

However, by all means use things like this as a feature to attract and retain staff.

- **No opposition in close proximity**

To have no competition close by is of obvious benefit, but what exactly is meant by "close proximity"? In this example close proximity meant about one hundred metres as there were four cafés within a five hundred metre radius.

- **This café has an excellent finish, a commercial kitchen and a stainless steel finish**

The standard of finish is aesthetically important, but obviously not a critical factor. A commercial kitchen is a must for any café. A stainless steel finish is easy to clean and beneficial.

It is impractical to use domestic appliances in cafés as they are not designed to stand up to the volume of use and the rough treatment of a working kitchen. Spend a few extra dollars to buy commercial appliances that are easier to clean and will stand the test of time.

- **Facing north to capture morning sun and has an outside terrace for smokers**

A sunny aspect is an added drawcard for customers so this is a good feature. On closer inspection the café was not found to be facing true North but North-east. Not a big issue, but this will affect the amount of sun received – as will any buildings in the immediate vicinity. If you need to check the aspect of the café, have a look at the café on Google Maps *(http://maps.google.com.au)*. Using the "street view" option on Google Maps can also be a good way to check the café's location without having to go there.

- **10-12 kg of coffee a week. Crema Bella blend**

The volume of coffee purchased is an important metric for analysis purposes. As coffee sales are typically 30-40% of total turnover, knowing the total coffee usage can give us a guide as to whether the total turnover is likely to be accurate.

Firstly you need to confirm that the volume of coffee stated in their business summary matches the volume purchased. You can do this by asking the vendor for copies of invoices from the coffee company. If possible average the coffee kilograms purchased over a period of 6 months, as coffee sales tend to drop in summer and increase in winter.

Next we can use this information to analyse the turnover.

A good rule of thumb is to estimate that 80 cups of coffee can be produced from each kilogram of coffee purchased. We can then estimate the total coffee revenue per week using a formula:

11 kilograms* x 80 cups per kilogram x $3.20 per cup = $2,816 (per week)

Take the weekly average of coffee purchased

We can then use this figure to calculate what percentage of revenue the coffee sales comprise:

$2,816 ÷ $7,700 = 37%

In this example the percentage of coffee sales appears plausible. If the coffee sales are below 30% or above 40% further investigation should be undertaken.

Note: some cafés have a policy of using a double shot for each coffee or they can use larger than standard baskets. As a result these cafés are likely to purchase significantly higher amounts of coffee (usually double). In this case, divide the number of kilograms purchased by two before calculating your coffee sales percentage.

The brand of coffee being used is also important. Be sure to research the brand to identify:

- What other cafés use this brand (ask them if they recommend the blend as well as the coffee company)
- Whether it has won any awards
- What people think of the brand.

Don't be afraid to contact the coffee company to find out more about them, but remember that you cannot disclose any details about the café you are looking at buying.

- **A three-month bank guarantee is required**

A bank guarantee allows you to provide a guarantee of payment to secure the lease. In the event that you were unable to meet the lease repayments the financial institution would pay (in this instance) three months rent to the landlord.

Typically you will be required to provide a security deposit or a sum of money as guarantee. One-off and ongoing bank fees may also apply – so be sure to consider these costs as part of your financial planning.

- **Voted in top ten breakfast cafés by Hungry Magazine**

Positive reviews and awards are always good, but don't take them at face value. Find out:

- When they received the award – if the award was 10 years ago it's unlikely to add much value to the business today
- Is the review or award from a reputable magazine or website?
- What locations did the review cover? Best breakfast café in the café's local suburb is very different to the best breakfast café in Australia

- Conversely, have they had any negative reviews recently?

Term Of Lease: 5 x 5

The term of this lease is 5 years with an option to extend for another 5 years. This means that you have a potential timeframe of 10 years to own the business at the premises. This is a good lease term as it gives you a solid timeframe in which to grow the business. You should also double check if the lease is new or existing – a new lease may mean that you have to pay GST on the purchase price of the business (a significant amount to pay up-front, although you will get it back).

Commencement Date: On negotiation

Much like the settlement date when buying a house, the date at which you take over (commencement) can be negotiated.

Increases/Reviews: 4% plus outgoings Strata Levy $1,532 per annum, Council Rates $1,564 per annum, Water rates $373 per quarter, 3-month Bank Guarantee

As mentioned previously, increases will commonly be factored into the lease. Here we see that the increase in this lease is 4% per annum. If we consider that the rent is $924 a week (including GST), this equates to $48,048 per annum. This correlates with the figure of $43,690 in the accounts (ex GST).

But back to the 4%. The following table shows the effect that a % increase in rent can have on the % of turnover. At the start of the lease the turnover amount is towards the higher end of the scale (10-15%), but if we make the assumption that turnover stays the same, over the period of 5 years rent as a percentage of turnover becomes very high. This means that you need to keep building the turnover over 5 years to avoid this increasing cost cutting into the profitability of the business.

	Total Lease Amount	4% Increase	Rent as % of Static Turnover
Start of Lease	$48,048	$1,922	14%
Year 1	$49,970	$1,999	14%
Year 2	$51,969	$2,079	15%
Year 3	$54,047	$2,162	15%
Year 4	$56,209	$2,248	16%
Year 5	$58,458	$2,338	17%

However, to be more accurate we should also include the strata and council rates in these figures:

	Total Lease Amount	4% Increase	Council Rates	Strata	As a % of Static Turnover
Start of Lease	$48,048	$1,922	$1,564	$1,532	15%
Year 1	$49,970	$1,999	$1,564	$1,532	16%
Year 2	$51,969	$2,079	$1,564	$1,532	16%
Year 3	$54,047	$2,162	$1,564	$1,532	17%
Year 4	$56,209	$2,248	$1,564	$1,532	18%
Year 5	$58,458	$2,338	$1,564	$1,532	18%

This scenario makes the assumption that strata rates and council rates stay constant over the 5 year period, which is unlikely. You can already start to see what an impact the rent will have on the profitability of the business over time. In this case the rent is initially high, but will increase to levels that may make it hard for the café to remain profitable.

Staff

Full-time Owner(s)	1
Casual Owner(s)	1
Full-time Staff	1
Casual Staff	5

Obtaining a copy of a detailed roster will help to identify how many staff are working in the business. You should reconcile the information in the roster with the information in the business summary. However, the ultimate test is to observe the business and to identify who is working in it. When you do this try to listen to the owner mentioning the staff member's name and write down all the names you hear and reconcile the names against the numbers / names in the roster and business summary. Ideally visit on a few different days (most cafés employ a few casual staff that work a couple of days a week).

In this particular example there were two main owners of the business. The main owner declared that he was the only person that worked full-time in the business while his wife, "the casual owner" worked "a few hours a week". On further observation this was found to be untrue as she was working in the business full-time, and also working 12 hours a week of her time as the chef (the highest paid position within the business).

Looking at things logically, if two people were to purchase this business they could slot in to cover the hours of both owners, but not the role of the chef. However, based on a sole owner of the business you'd have to pay staff to replace the casual owner.

Note: The café opened for 48 weeks of the year, closing

for 4 weeks at Christmas. Make sure you account for any weeks closed in your calculations.

Let's add that up:

12 hrs x $30 per hr = $360 per wk x 48 wks = **$17,280 per yr**
40 hrs x $15 per hr = $600 per wk x 48 wks = **$28,800 per yr**
Total to fill 12 hours of chef work + 40 hours of waitstaff work per annum = **$46,080**

Superannuation at 9% = **$4,147**

Total "backfill" amount = $50,227

Suddenly this doesn't look like such a good business to buy as the $50,000 will be coming straight off the profit.

But wait, there's more! On observation it was discovered that the main owner was working 6 days a week! And he was buying all the fruit and vegetables himself from the markets!

Now, many café owners really do work very hard, but I would suggest that if you want to be able to build your business by working on it (not in it) you need to be able to give yourself time to do this. If you work 6 days a week all you will be doing is operating it. The business will have little potential to grow. It's a bit like the difference between a plant that just survives by getting rainwater or the plant that you regularly water. You need to take time out to water the plant to help it grow.

> *When I ran my café I made sure that I spent time working "on the business" not just in the business. Working "on the business" I spent time to do work that would help to grow the business, such as newsletter drops, coffee promotions and visiting local businesses – rather than just working "in the business" which refers to the day-to-day running of the café.*

Asking Price: $120,000

Usually the broker will advise the seller on what the asking price should be. The simple rule is, the higher the profit, the higher the price. It's a very inexact science and often some cafés buck the trend completely (such as franchised businesses which are initially very expensive to set up and hence are more expensive when it comes to selling them). How vendors or brokers value cafés often comes down to considering recent similar sales (similar to how real estate agents set house prices).

Factors that influence the asking price include:

- Current profit
- Franchise / non-franchise
- Location, i.e. busy / not busy
- Length of lease remaining
- Potential of business.

Tips:

- Never pay the asking price – always consider it to be the "top" price and your aim is to negotiate down
- Ask your accountant for his opinion on the valuation
- If in doubt get a licenced business valuer to assess the business
- As an overall tip, when looking to buy a café, begin by considering 5 possible businesses. By doing this you are comparing a range of options. For your information, in Sydney alone there are several hundred cafés or takeaways available for sale at any one time!

Stock: $2,000

Stock includes everything that comprises the cost of goods – food, drinks, napkins, etc. It does not include fixtures and fittings or equipment. The stock estimate is just that – an estimate. Budget for double the stock amount, just in case. You'd be surprised at what café owners can find at the back of cupboards and drystores. In this case $2,000 is a fairly typical amount for a small café such as this one.

Financial Projections: based on a weekly turnover of $7,700

In this section the turnover will be stated. This will be

the figure that the café will have to achieve in the trial period if the sale is to progress. We'll talk about the trial period later.

Be thorough with your analysis when dealing with "projections", as projected figures have been altered to show how the business *might* perform in the future.

Operating Expenses: Outgoings

Outgoings	$88.00
Rent	$924.00
TOTAL OPERATING EXPENSES	$1,012.00

Outgoings represent other costs associated with the building in which the café is located – for example strata fees, maintenance fees, storage fees or possibly even marketing fees (e.g. for shopping centres). Rent is obviously the amount payable as per the lease.

Utilities

Utilities include gas, electricity, water, etc. Unlike renting a residential property, utilities such as water will not be included in your rent. If you are renting a business within a strata complex there are several other factors to consider.

Strata

Strata is basically a means of managing building and expenses associated with the building that a number of premises are a part of. Basically the members of the strata are required to pay fees (usually based on the size of premises) to maintain the overall building. In return they have a say in the goings on of the strata from a maintenance, repair and construction point of view. Strata will add to your costs (outgoings). Your landlord will usually add the strata fees to your lease agreement.

There are a number of factors to bear in mind when buying a café in a strata block:

- Major expenses are shared with all the strata units, i.e. special levies. These are generally uncommon, but may be more prevalent in older strata blocks
- Facilities such as toilets or storage facilities may be shared with other businesses or tenants
- In bigger strata schemes, e.g. shopping centres, there may be marketing fees payable
- The physical exterior of the premises (e.g. windows & walls) are covered by strata insurance – the inside is not. This means, for example, if a window is broken strata will pay to have the window repaired.

Due to the regulations surrounding the management of strata blocks there is always a good level of detail available regarding the running of the strata scheme and the finances involved.

Strata levies are generally paid quarterly and the levies are split into two:

- The administration fund – which covers day-to-day running costs of the strata
- The sinking fund – which is money put aside to cover the long term repair costs of the strata as it gets older.

Prior to buying a café in a strata block you should check:

- The last 12-24 months of documentation including all meetings, AGMs (annual general meetings), EGMs (emergency general meetings)
- Financial reports on the condition of the administration and sinking funds
- Whether any special levies are due to be put in place.

An Analysis of the Financials

In this example we have used the "true" historical figures rather than figures that have been altered to show "projections" or assumptions.

The first table shows the actual details provided by the vendor's accountant; the second table shows an analysis of those financials.

If you'd like to test your learning so far, analyse the financials on the next 3 pages, then compare your notes to the analysis on the following page.

Financials from Vendor's Accountant

	Prior Year	Projected	Vendor Comments
Sales	$349,022	$349,022	
Total Income	$349,022	$349,022	
Food General	$91,792	$91,792	
Total Cost of Sales	$91,782	$91,782	
Gross Profit	$257,240	$257,240	
EXPENSES			
Advertising	$902	$902	
Bank Charges	$1,975	$1,975	
Contractors	$50,586	$50,586	
Dues & Subscriptions	$1,340	$1,340	
Insurance	$5,949	$5,949	
Laundry and Cleaning	$1,406	$1,406	
Lease Payment - Car	$5,298	―――――	Add Back.
Legal & Accounting	$8,301	$4,315	Add Back.

	Prior Year	Projected	Vendor Comments
Maintenance	$4,357	$4,357	
General Expenses	$2,165	$2,165	
Petrol	$547	————	Add Back.
Other Fees	$273	$273	
Kitchen Supplies	$3,403	$3,403	
Superannuation	$2,723	$2,723	
Wages & Salaries	$46,158	$17,160	Add Back - Owners' Wages.
Postage	$70	$70	
Rent	$36,400	$45,244	Market Rent & Rates.
Outgoings/Strata Fees	$1,580	$1,580	
Stationery	$515	$515	
Rubbish Removal	$915	$915	
Telephone	$1,325	$1,325	
Training Costs	$109	$109	

Analysing The Business Summary - An Example

	Prior Year	Projected	Vendor Comments
Uniforms	$769	----------	Add Back.
Electricity	$4,061	$4,061	
Gas	$1,074	$1,074	
Water	$391	$391	
TOTAL EXPENSES	$182,914	$151,840	
Operating Profit	$74,326	$105,400	
Other Income			
Interest Income	$1,163	$1,163	
TOTAL OTHER INCOME	$1,163	$1,163	
NET PROFIT / LOSS	$75,489	$106,563	

Analysis of Financials

	Prior Year	Analysis
Sales	$349,022	
Total Income	$349,022	$7,271 per week based on 48 weeks per year open.
Food General	$91,792	The food cost has not been separated from the other related food costs in this case.
Total Cost of Sales	$91,782	26% of total sales.
Gross Profit	$257,240	
EXPENSES		
Advertising	$902	Ask what forms of advertising they are using. This is a small amount so it is unlikely that they are performing regular advertising.
Bank Charges	$1,975	Fairly standard amount.
Contractors	$50,586	Who is this for? Chefs? Check invoices to back this up. What is the hourly rate? Contractors are unlikely to be paid superannuation.
Dues & Subscriptions	$1,340	Check what this is for – memberships to associations? Magazine subscriptions?
Insurance	$5,949	Seems a little high so check what coverage is in place.
Laundry and Cleaning	$1,406	Laundry seems unnecessary for a café of this size – could be a personal expense.
Lease Payment - Car	$5,298	A reasonable amount for a car lease – if you own your own car you can save some money here. If not you need to factor in costs of a new car.
Legal & Accounting	$8,301	Very high which indicates that the vendor could have had some legal issues – well worth finding out.

Analysing The Business Summary - An Example

	Prior Year	Analysis
Maintenance	$4,357	Seems high – could be a sign of ageing equipment in need of repair or replacement.
General Expenses	$2,165	A very vague category – questions should be asked as to what this is.
Petrol	$547	Seems a very low amount considering that the owners drive to and from the café each day.
Other Fees	$273	What are these fees?
Kitchen Supplies	$3,403	Again – this is vague and could be used to hide further equipment repairs.
Superannuation	$2,723	Difficult to check if this is correct as some employees who only work a small amount are not entitled to superannuation, but this figure should never exceed 9% of wages.
Wages & Salaries	$46,158	This amount equates to the wage of just over one person which seems a small amount. This could indicate that the owners are paying staff cash.
Postage	$70	What postage?
Rent	$36,400	Rent is due to increase to $45,244 – an increase of almost $9,000.
Outgoings/Strata Fees	$1,580	Double check what this includes – remember that strata rates vary from year-to-year and do not include special levies.
Stationery	$515	Clarify – for menu printing? Marketing materials?
Garbage Removal	$915	Garbage removal is generally charged per bin emptied. This value seems a little low so it is worth asking if they dispose of their garbage themselves.
Telephone	$1,325	Is there a landline? Does the owner have a mobile phone?
Training Costs	$109	What staff training is undertaken?

	Prior Year	Analysis
Uniforms	$769	Is there a staff uniform?
Electricity	$4,061	This is fairly typical for a café of this size.
Gas	$1,074	This is fairly typical for a café of this size.
Water	$391	This seems low – ask to see invoices.
TOTAL EXPENSES	$182,914	
Operating Profit	$74,326	Profit is 21% which is fairly good for a café.
Other Income		If there is other income stated e.g. other sales, be sure to ask where this income is coming from.
Interest Income	$1,163	This is likely to be personal income from bank accounts and therefore should be discarded from the profit.
TOTAL OTHER INCOME	$1,163	

The next stage to our analysis is to apply these financials to the situation of the new buyer. As we discussed earlier, if this café is to be run by one person, additional wages would be required. As we also know, the rent will be increasing by approximately $9k per annum. There are also some interest earnings that may not apply. So when we look at our figures in light of these facts we see an altogether different picture of the business:

NET PROFIT / LOSS	$75,489	
Wages required to cover 1 owner	$50,000	Based on 40 hours per week with dual role as chef.
Increase in rent	$9,000	Increase in rental as per new lease.
Interest income	$1,163	Not applicable.
ESTIMATED PROFIT	$15,326	4% profit margin - NOT GOOD!

What initially looked like a highly profitable business now looks somewhat different. If we also assume that our new owner had to borrow the $120,000, this would equate to a loan repayment of approximately $7k per annum, thereby reducing the profit to $8k per annum.

There are several key lessons in this, most importantly:

- Use only accurate historical figures as the basis for your calculations
- Ignore "add-backs" – these are business costs, but costs which provide the owner with a financial benefit e.g. the owner leasing his car via the business
- Update figures to represent your personal situation
- Don't forget about borrowing costs.

Other Useful Information

BAS Returns

BAS Returns (Business Activity Statement Returns) are a great source of information about a café. Business activity statements are usually completed quarterly throughout the year – commonly known as Q1, Q2, Q3 & Q4. The following fields on the BAS Return are of particular interest:

BAS Return Field	How to use this information
ABN (Australian Business Number)	This can be used to identify the entity that owns the café. The ABN can then be used to perform the online ASIC search (see next section "Information Online").
Total Sales	Total sales display the revenue per quarter. The sum of all 4 quarters should equal the total revenue as reported in the end-of-year financials. This is the total amount to which GST is applicable. Seeing a breakdown of sales into Q1-4 can be useful as it can show variances in trade throughout the year due to seasonality, e.g. winter may be busier than summer.
GST on Sales or GST Instalment	This is the standard 10% payable upon sales. This should equal 10% of turnover.
Capital Purchases	This represents purchases of items of a capital nature not related to the cost of goods, e.g. equipment.
Non-capital Purchases	This represents the cost of goods and should be approximately 30% of turnover. This figure should not vary significantly throughout the year. Any large variances throughout the year should be questioned.
GST on Purchases	This is the amount that can be claimed back (deducted) from the GST payable. This amount should be approximately 2-3% of turnover and includes GST on purchases such as rent.
Total Salary Wages and other payments	This is a useful figure as it shows the total wages paid per quarter. Again, this should tie up with the wages figures reported in the financials. Also the % figure for wages should be roughly consistent across each quarter, e.g. approx 25-35% of turnover.

Information Online

ASIC

The ASIC (the Australian Securities and Investments Commission) website at *http://www.asic.gov.au* has an online facility where you can check company details *(http://www.search.asic.gov.au)*. You can search using a variety of different information including ACN / ABN or even the business name. There are many reasons why this can be a useful facility to check as it can provide information on:

- Ownership of company
- Registered business names linked to companies
- Documents / requests provided to ASIC.

This service can help to identify the owners of the business as often owners use personal names in the company names. For example, if you do a search on the café name "Smith's Café" and it leads you to a business name of "Smith & Jones Pty Ltd", then it could be that there are two owners of the business. If this café is being sold as being run by "one owner", questions should be asked about how involved the other owner is in the process.

Another example of the usefulness of ASIC search is when more than one business is linked to a company.

For example, a company could own a catering business as well as a café – let's call them "John's Catering" and "John's Café".

John's Café has a turnover of $300k per annum and "John's Catering" has a turnover of $200k per annum. On the company accounts for "John's Holdings Ltd" it displays a turnover of $500k per annum. So when you come along looking to buy "John's Café", you look at the figures and see $500k turnover per annum and think that you are getting a great business; but disaster! You've just bought a $300k per annum business instead of a $500k per annum one. It pays to do a thorough search to determine if a 1-1 relationship exists between the registered business name and the company.

Food Authorities

Recently, the NSW government implemented a "name and shame" list for hospitality businesses that have been fined for contravening food hygiene laws. Unfortunately, other states around Australia have yet to implement similar lists. But if you are buying a café in NSW, the list can be a useful source of information.

Would you buy a café that was fined for having rats in the kitchen? Do the seals on the fridges contravene safety laws and need to be replaced? More importantly, how would appearing on the "name and shame" list affect the café's reputation and future custom? Worth knowing.

http://www.foodauthority.nsw.gov.au

Café Reviews

Other useful sources of information on the Internet are café review websites such as *www.eatability.com.au*. Not only can these websites give you an idea as to how well the business is / has performed but they can also provide "nuggets" of information that can be useful in your analysis. For example, the review may mention an owner's name or the name of a particularly friendly waitress. They can help to point out good or bad service and dishes that delight or disappoint.

> *On several occasions I have discovered businesses advertised for sale as "Five day a week businesses", but after looking at review sites on the internet I have found that they have been trading several nights a week or one or two days on a weekend. Averaging the turnover over 5 days then makes the business look more profitable than it actually is.*

Decision Time

For each café business summary you look at it's important to make an initial decision based on the financials. Don't waste time at this stage – dismiss those that don't add up and be quick to identify those that look like good prospects. Next you need to get out and look.

Assessing The Location

OK, so you've done a thorough analysis of the business summary and have identified a few cafés to look at. The next stage is to go and have a quick look at the café (or, as we mentioned earlier, first check it out on Google maps).

Use the following checklist as a guide to your first visit. Remember that this is just a quick check to decide whether you want to look into things in more detail, but it is an important stage in the process.

Location
- How busy is the location?
- Are there many local businesses nearby?
- Is there a lot of passing trade?
- Is the location pleasant?

Competition
- How many other cafés are in the area?
- Are competitors similar to the café?
- How are competitors priced in comparison?

> *Competition is not always bad! Enough cafés or restaurants in the one area can create an "eat street" which attracts passionate food lovers in droves.*

Café Analysis

- Is it busy?
- Does it have indoor / outdoor seating?
- Does it have an interesting menu?
- Is service prompt, friendly and efficient?
- Is the food good?
- Do the staff seem happy?
- Are the owners present? (This may be difficult to tell, but look for the person usually giving the orders!)

You!

Ask yourself if you can see yourself working there. Are you excited by the opportunity?

Customer Patterns

If the drive-by analysis looks good it is worthwhile to look at the business several times throughout the course of the buying process. Try to identify:

- When peak periods are
- When quiet periods are
- Whether trade is mostly sit-in or take-away.

If you can, count the number of customers per hour over a few different time periods to get an understanding of how busy the café is.

> *Generally most cafés have three peak periods:*
> - *Breakfast 8-10 a.m.*
> - *Lunch 12-2 p.m.*
> - *Dinner 7-9 p.m.*

Trade will generally be significantly higher during these periods so be sure to visit the café in both peak and off-peak periods to understand how much the level of trade fluctuates.

This is usually enough of an analysis to give you an idea of whether or not the description in the business summary matches reality. If, after conducting the initial visit you are still interested, then the next stage is to arrange a meeting with the owner of the café to thoroughly assess the business.

Meeting The Owner

When you have decided that you are interested in the café you should make an appointment to meet the owner(s). This is usually arranged by the business broker. The business broker may or may not attend. It is better to meet the owner of the café on their own if possible as they are likely to be more honest. Business brokers tend to put "spin" on the owner's words and shield them from difficult questions. However, always direct your questions at the owner and watch their body language if the business broker answers for them. Once the broker has arranged a suitable time for you to meet, you will start to get organised for the meeting.

The Grilling

The purpose of the meeting with the owner is not just to ask questions about the café – it is to find the truth about the café. Consider your role to be like a lawyer cross-examining a witness on the stand.

Tips:

- Ask as many questions as you like. If your questions are reasonable, you should expect answers

- Not answering questions is a sure sign of the owners hiding something

- If there are two owners, try to arrange two separate

meetings with them and ask the same questions to see if their responses differ!

- Take a second person along as the note taker. This allows you to maintain eye contact with the owner and to watch what is happening around the café. The second person may hear things differently to you

- Ask the broker why the owner is selling and ask the owner separately

- If you are making an "official" visit to see the café and to ask the owner questions, make this "formal" by carrying a note pad and reading your questions. At the end, thank the owner and put your notes away. The owner may then feel that the "interview" is over. Once their guard is dropped, they may tell you other useful information.

Key Questions

The owner may be nervous, so begin with something easy to allow them to relax. You could ask them to walk you through their typical day in 5 minutes, so they are talking about something familiar.

The following pages contain a list of key questions and what you should look for in the owner's answers.

General Questions

Question	What to look for
Are you the only owner of the business?	Identify number of owners – if you are a single buyer they may try to show that the business can be run profitably by one owner so they may not be keen to admit that it is run by two owners.
Do you have any family working in the business?	Try to identify any staff paid cash or not paid at all – family working in the business but not claiming a wage (on paper) can make the business look more profitable than it actually is.
Why are you selling the business?	Check the response against the broker's response. Try to drill down and obtain more information where they give a "general" response.
How long have you owned the business?	If the timeframe is short it may indicate that they have made a mistake buying the business. If the timeframe is longer it shows that the business is likely to be a more stable operation.
How many hours a week / days per week do you spend working in the business hands-on?	This is very important as it will determine the number of hours that need to be "replaced" by the new owner(s). Be sure to cross-reference this number with the numbers in the roster.
Opening / closing times? Breakfast / Lunch / Dinner 7 days?	Remember that a café opening 60 hours a week and earning $8,000 a week is a more profitable business than a café opening 80 hours a week and earning $8,000 a week. Calculate the $ per hour. Ensure you check the opening hours against the business summary and information on the Internet.

Financial Questions

Question	What to look for
What is the average turnover per week?	Compare the response to the business summary. Ask about variations of turnover throughout the year (seasonality). Ask if this does or does not include any cash not declared.
What are your food costs per week?	Compare this to your financial analysis – if there is variation, ask why!
What are your staff costs per week?	Compare this to your analysis of the roster – ask if it includes owners' or family members' wages or staff paid by cash.
What is the rent per week?	Check against the business summary – ask what the additional outgoings and strata rates are.
How much profit do you make per week?	Check against the business summary – if it is different ask them to explain why it is different.

Staff Questions

Question	What to look for
How many chefs do you have? Casual? Full-time?	There should be more than one chef in order to provide cover. Casual chefs will be more expensive. Determine if any of the owners do any of the cooking.
How many staff? What is the break up? – full-time, part-time, etc	Determine exact numbers of: waitstaff, baristas, chefs, kitchen hands. Determine whether each of these staff are full-time, part-time or casual. Compare with roster information.
How many staff are on, on a typical weekday / weekend?	Compare this with your observational information / roster information. Watch for indications that the staffing is different to what you have observed.
What rates do you currently pay staff?	Obtain pay rates for all staff. Use this to populate the roster to calculate weekly staff costs – compare this to the business summary.
Do you have a sample roster?	If they haven't provided this already ask for it. If they do not have one, ask what days / hours each staff member works.
Is there a staff handbook or operational guide?	Most cafés are unlikely to have one of these (unless they are a franchise), but it is worth asking as it may help you to run the café easier in the future.
Who runs the café when you are not available?	It is an advantage when you buy a café to have someone who knows what they are doing and who can take the pressure off you – so if there is someone who fits this description, find out who they are and keep them happy!

Supplier Questions

Question	What to look for
What suppliers do you currently use? Do you buy any stock yourself?	Identify who their key suppliers are and how many supply direct to the premises. If the owners buy a large amount of stock themselves and you are not able to maintain this, you can expect your food costs to rise.
How many kilos of coffee are you using per week?	This can be a useful way to verify turnover. An average café will be able to get 80 cups of coffee out of a kilo of coffee beans. Multiply the amount of kilos by 80 cups per kilo then multiply this by the price of an average cup of coffee to calculate the total coffee revenue per week. This will typically represent about 40% of turnover.
Size of coffee basket being used?	The size of the basket will determine the amount of cups per kilo. Some cafés use larger baskets to improve the quality of the coffee. The larger the basket the less cups per kilo – therefore the cost per cup increases.
Are all suppliers set up on credit terms?	This may help to identify whether or not suppliers are being paid cash and hence if the café is taking a large amount of cash or not.

Trade Questions

Question	What to look for
How has the level of revenue changed since you have owned the business?	This should be verified against any long-term figures you have, e.g. financials for last three years.
What effect does seasonality have on the business – summer versus winter?	This will help you to get a feel for when turnover is at its highest. Compare this to when the café is being sold – are they selling it at the highest revenue period to make it easier to get through the trial period?
How often do you update / alter the menu?	This can give an indication of how well the business is run or whether the café is in decline. The longer the time between menu changes, the more likely the owners have lost interest in the business and hence it may be in decline.

Competitor Questions

Question	What to look for
Who are your main competitors? How do you rate them?	Although you should undertake your own analysis of competitors, it is valuable to get an insight from the current owners as to whom they think represents the biggest threat.
How has the area changed since you started running the business?	This can be important as it can show potential growth opportunities, i.e. new housing developments.
How do your competitors' prices compare to yours?	This will help you to understand the café's pricing positioning in comparison to competitors and to decide if changes should be made.

Marketing Questions

Question	What to look for
What marketing have you undertaken for the business? How successful were these initiatives?	Answers to this question will show how much the owners work "on the business" instead of "in the business" – this can help to identify whether there is potential to improve by doing concerted marketing.
What continual marketing / promotions do you perform?	It is good to understand what commitments they have made to marketing and what benefit they believe this has had for the café.
What forms of customer research have you / do you employ?	Do they use questionnaires or comment cards? This shows their level of commitment to understanding the customer.
What is your pricing strategy?	Premium pricing? Low pricing, high volume? It's important to know what their pricing strategy has been so you can identify potential to improve.

Maintenance Questions

Question	What to look for
What repairs have you performed in the last 12 months?	There are likely to be some repairs every year – this is not a great concern. Unless the café is new, an owner telling you that they have had no repairs is a highly unlikely scenario. Look for any repairs that may point to bigger, more expensive problems such as plumbing or refrigeration.
How often do you clean the range hood?	This is a good question to test their standards of cleanliness. The commitment to cleanliness is a good reflection of how much they care for the café and the customers. The range hood should be cleaned at least once a month, but note that not every café has a range hood (which can limit the type of food allowed to be cooked).
How often is the grease trap emptied? When was the last empty?	The grease trap (if they have one) should be emptied roughly every 6 months. Find out when it was emptied so that you know when it will be required to be emptied next. Also ask how much they currently pay and who provides the service.

Premises Questions

Question	What to look for
How many seats inside and outside?	Count the number of seats to verify the business summary numbers. Is there potential for better arrangement of the seats or extra seating?
What is the current rent / terms of the lease?	Cross reference with the business summary / financials. Check if the rent figure includes GST. Check how long is left on the lease and if there is an option to extend.
Will the lease be a new lease?	Check if the lease will be a new lease (this may have GST implications).
Is there an option on the lease?	There should be an option on the lease – the longer the option, the greater the security.
Are there any clauses in the lease, e.g. development clause?	Whilst not standard, it is worth asking to identify any special conditions within the lease that may add extra cost.
What are the other outgoings?	Other outgoings should include strata fees or any other shared fees, etc.
When is rent reviewed?	Again any rent increases should correspond with the outgoings in the business summary.
What are the percentage yearly increases in rent?	This is normally a fixed percentage and wouldn't normally be higher than 5%.
Is the building a strata building?	If so, ask who the managing agents are and how you can get reports on the strata. Can they give you contact details of the managing agent?

Premises Questions - continued

Question	What to look for
Who is the landlord?	What does the landlord do? Do they try to involve themselves in the business? How do they currently pay them? A good landlord is one that you never see or hear from!
How is your relationship with the landlord?	Look for any signs of negativity towards the landlord – this can indicate that the landlord may cause trouble.
Is there a parking space?	Ideally there should be a parking space near to the café. If there isn't one, it isn't the end of the world, but having one will make your life easier.

Licensing / Regulatory questions

Question	What to look for
What are the approved council hours of trade?	Ask to see the council documents showing the approved hours of trade. The current opening hours must be within the approved hours of trade.
What type of liquor licence do you hold?	If they do hold a liquor licence, verify if there are any restrictions on it. Check if you need to apply for a new licence.
Any other licences held?	For example, footpath permission licence for tables and chairs. How much are these licences?
Are fire regulations complied with? e.g. fire extinguishers?	Check that fire blankets and fire extinguishers are in place. Check that emergency exit signs are in place. Check that fire extinguishers have been checked every six months by a licensed company.

Key Question Template

You can use the blank templates on the following pages to enter the owner's answers to the questions.

Tip: photocopy for re-use!

General Questions

Question	Response
Are you the only owner of the business?	
Do you have any family working in the business?	
Why are you selling the business?	
How long have you owned the business?	
How many hours a week / days per week do you spend working in the business hands on?	
Opening / closing times? Breakfast / Lunch / Dinner 7 days?	

Financial Questions

Question	Response
What is the average turnover per week?	
What are your food costs per week?	
What are your staff costs per week?	
What is the rent per week?	
How much profit do you make per week?	

Staff Questions

Question	Response
How many chefs do you have? Casual? Full-time?	
How many staff? What is the break up – full-time, part-time, etc?	
How many staff are on, on a typical weekday / weekend?	
What rates do you currently pay staff?	
Do you have a sample roster?	
Is there a staff handbook or operational guide?	

Staff Questions - continued

Question	Response
Who runs the café when you are not available?	

Supplier Questions

Question	Response
What suppliers do you currently use? Do you buy any stock yourself?	
How many kilos of coffee are you using per week?	
Are all suppliers set up on credit terms?	

Trade Questions

Question	Response
How has the level of revenue changed since you have owned the business?	
What effect does seasonality have on the business – summer versus winter?	
How often do you update / alter the menu?	

Competitor Questions

Question	Response
Who are your main competitors? How do you rate them?	
How has the area changed since you started running the business?	
How do your competitors' prices compare to yours?	

Marketing Questions

Question	Response
What marketing have you undertaken for the business? How successful were these initiatives?	
What continual marketing / promotions do you perform?	
What forms of customer research have you / do you employ?	
What is your pricing strategy?	

Maintenance Questions

Question	Response
What repairs have you performed in the last 12 months?	
How often do you clean the range hood?	
How often is the grease trap emptied? When was the last empty?	

Premises Questions

Question	Response
How many seats inside and outside?	
What is the current rent / terms of the lease?	
Will the lease be a new lease?	
Is there an option on the lease?	
Are there any clauses in the lease, e.g. development clause?	
What are the other outgoings?	

Premises Questions - continued

Question	Response
When is rent reviewed?	
What are the percentage yearly increases in rent?	
Is the building a strata building?	
Who is the landlord?	
How is your relationship with the landlord?	
Is there a parking space?	

Licensing / Regulatory questions

Question	Response
What are the approved council hours of trade?	
What type of liquor licence do you hold?	
Any other licences held?	
Are fire regulations complied with? e.g. fire extinguishers?	

Analysis Techniques

Once you have gathered all your information it can be a good idea to sit down and do a detailed analysis. This can help to crystallise your thoughts and can be a useful start to a business plan if you do decide to buy the café.

Two fast and easy ways to do this are to use these analysis techniques:

- The Four "P's" (Product, Price, Place, Promotion)
- SWOT Analysis (Strengths, Weaknesses, Opportunities, Threats)

Examples of these two methods can be found on the following pages.

The Four "P's" – An example

Product – Menu design:	Menu has a strong emphasis on Mediterranean cuisine. Pasta, risotto, etc. Café Mocha is highly rated for its breakfast items and its perfectly cooked eggs. It was named as 1 of the top 10 breakfast cafés in the city by Hungry magazine. However, the physical design of the menu is misleading and does not maximise sales. There is also no exterior menu to attract passing trade. There are no bundled (combo) menu options.
Price	Pricing is relative to the affluence of the area – not cheap but not expensive. (Eggs Mocha, for example – 2 poached eggs, tomato concasse, pesto sauce on Turkish bread costs $14.50). A coffee is $3.20.
Place	Location is excellent, on the main street in Pleasantville, adjacent to high traffic shopping strips. The physical fit-out of the café is in good order with a minimalist "trendy" design. There are 22 seats inside, with 18 on a sunny patio outside. It is North facing to catch the maximum amount of sun.
Promotion	There are numerous promotional options: • Increased advertising (with editorial) • Free food & coffee sampling • Coffee promotions / prize draws • Leaflet drops • Special events • Charity promotions • Deals for small businesses • Loyalty deals.

SWOT Analysis – An example

Strengths	• Location • Good trade (growing) • Low cost of goods • Negligible competition (unlikely to change short-term).
Weaknesses	• Small number of seats (limited revenue) • Dependence on key staff • Part of strata scheme • Café trend changing from minimalism towards comfort.
Opportunities	• Open 7 days • Open peak evenings • Obtain liquor licence (no toilets is a problem) • Bundle product offerings to maximise sales • Promote more effectively.
Threats	• Increasing prices in area – increased rent • Entry of similar competition.

The following pages contain some blank templates for you to use.

Tip: photocopy for re-use!

The Four "P's" – Template

Product

Price

Place

Promotion

SWOT Analysis – Template

Strengths
Weaknesses
Opportunities
Threats

Council Documents

Every café requires council authorisation to trade as a café. This is called the "Permitted Use". The permitted use documentation will also include details of the opening hours approved by council. Ask your solicitor to obtain these documents either from the broker or from the local council. These documents are extremely important to confirm that the café is legally allowed to trade and the permitted hours of trade. The trading hours are particularly relevant if you are considering expanding the café's trading hours in the future, e.g. opening for dinner.

Legal Documentation

When you have decided upon a café to buy it is essential that a qualified solicitor looks at all the documentation. This should include:

- The lease
- The strata documentation (if applicable)
- The council documentation
- The contract (of sale)
- Any other relevant documentation.

Negotiations

So, you're ready to make an offer. Let's recap on valuations from our business summary example.

Factors that influence the asking price include:

- Current profit
- Franchise / non-franchise
- Location, i.e. busy / not busy
- Length of lease remaining
- Potential of business.

Tips:

- Never pay the asking price – always consider it to be the "top" price and your aim is to negotiate down
- Ask your accountant for his opinion on the valuation
- If in doubt get a licenced business valuer to assess the business
- As an overall tip, when looking to buy a café, begin by considering five possible businesses. By doing this you are comparing a range of options.

Considering all that, the next step is to put your offer forward to the business broker directly. Just like with any sales situation the broker may try to put pressure on you and use "sales tactics" to get the best price for his vendor. Try not to let heart rule head at this time and don't be rushed into making increased offers.

> *Often I see brokers indulging in a number of tactics to try to increase offers or rush buyers into committing to an offer. Here are some examples of what they may tell you:*
>
> - *"We have a number of people looking to buy this café"*
> - *"We will supply all the financials after an offer is accepted"*
> - *"This café won't last long – it's a bargain"*
> - *"If you make an offer we'll take it off the market".*
>
> *I have seen buyers make emotional decisions that have led them to pay tens of thousands of dollars over the asking price. It's not a time to rush into a decision – it's time to keep a cool head!*

Offer Acceptance

So finally you agree a price with the broker and the café is yours – or is it? The answer is, no, not yet. The café is only yours when you have signed the contract and paid the 10% deposit. Until that is completed there is no formal agreement and the vendor can still accept other offers if they wish.

Once you have agreed a price and all the legalities have been checked out by your solicitor you should aim to sign the contract and pay the deposit as quickly as possible to secure the business as your own.

> *Nothing is secured until the contract is signed and the 10% deposit is paid. Sometimes brokers will ask you to pay a small deposit (e.g. $1,000) once an offer is agreed – this is meaningless and gives you no security over the purchase of the café.*

The Trial & Settlement

The Trial

As we mentioned earlier the trial period occurs after you have agreed to buy the business and have paid a deposit. In this period you are not actively involved with running the business. You should be present for at least a full week, attending in the same hours as the owner to observe the business and sign off on the takings at the end of the day. The aim of the trial period is to ensure that the takings for that week are equal to or greater than the $ amount agreed with you (usually this is the weekly turnover specified in the business summary).

When watching the business during the trial period, try to look out for the following:

- Family or friends of the owners coming to the café that week to bolster the turnover

- The owner putting transactions through the till and paying for them using his own money.

It's difficult to be watching what goes into the till at all times so prior to the trial period ask your solicitor to add to the contract the requirement for transactional level "Z Reads" to be provided as well as hourly "Z Reads".

Note: A "Z Read" is a function on point of sale systems

that clears the transactions and prints a report. Z reads are typically performed at the end of the day's trade as part of "cashing up".

The one good thing that the trial period will give you is an opportunity to observe the goings on within the business. Think of yourself as a mystery diner, but on behalf of the other customers in the café. You should take careful note of the following:

Trial observation form:

Busy periods, e.g. more than 50% full (note times)	
Staff competency	
How many staff on at one time?	
Average wait time for customers to be served	
Average wait time for customers to receive drinks	
Average wait time for customers to receive food	
Type of staff working, e.g. barista / chef / waiters	
What tasks the owner is performing	
Days / hours worked by the owner	
What would you do differently?	

Even if this information does not seem immediately useful to you, it will help you later on when you are actively involved with running the business.

Training

During the trial period, learn as much as you can about the business from the owner. Try to get the owner to commit to a structured training plan where you learn about all facets of the business. For example:

- 1 day as kitchen hand
- 2 days as waiter
- 2 days as barista
- 2 days as cashier / manager.

This period is also the perfect time to document everything that the owner tells you and to develop this information into processes and procedures – in other words, an operations manual. This will be of huge benefit to you when running the business.

Settlement

When you sign the contract it will specify the date for settlement. Much like buying a property, settlement is a complex process involving the transfer of several legal documents and funds between parties. This will usually involve the vendor's solicitor and your solicitor meeting to perform the settlement.

Prior to settlement there are a number of tasks that you need to organise:

Update suppliers:

The suppliers may have no idea that the café has been for sale so you should call each of the café's suppliers to introduce yourself and to supply contact and payment details. At this point you should also ask them to send you any forms that you are required to complete – for example requests for credit. Ensure that you have documented all contact details for suppliers as well as their contact hours and delivery day / times.

Cheques for settlement:

Your solicitor will advise you on what cheques need to be prepared for settlement. These have to be bank cheques. Alternatively they may advise that you can pay by direct credit prior to the settlement date.

Cash float / change for point-of-sale system:

This is an amount of cash that is kept in the point-of-sale system so that you have adequate change to give customers. Usually this is $300 or so. You should also have a supply of change (coins) on hand in case you run out (also usually about $300). You can go to the bank and purchase this from them, but it may be easiest simply to buy the till float from the current owner (via cash / cheque).

Stocktake:

Prior to settlement day you will undertake a stocktake – this will involve going through all the current stock in the café and calculating a value of each item. These costs are then added up to give you a total valuation of stock (SAV as it is commonly referred to). When you do the stocktake keep an eye out for any stock which you think is unsatisfactory. At the end of the stocktake you will be required to pay the café owner directly by cash or cheque. Ensure that the owner provides a receipt for this.

Staff roster:

On settlement day it is your responsibility to ensure that you have staff available to work so you should ensure that you have contacted staff to work on the day and for the rest of the week. Ask the current owner for some help to do this. Ensure that you have current contact details for all staff.

Upon completion of settlement you will be notified by your solicitor that the settlement has taken place. You will then be the proud owner of a café and your great new adventure is just beginning…

A Day In The Life Of A Café Owner

Every café is a bit different, but there are similarities in all of them – food, coffee, service and hard work! For the benefit of those reading this that haven't yet set foot in a café other than to eat and drink, the following chapter is for you. It is a summary of my experiences of a "typical" day as a café owner.

The alarm clock rings. I wake and sit in bed for a few minutes planning another successful day – ticking off all the things I have done and creating a new mental checklist of all the things I have to do today.

I swing my legs out of bed and go to the bathroom and quickly shower. I am always organised and punctual in the mornings so that I can get to the café and take my time opening up. I dress in one of my daily café outfits: black t-shirt with the coffee company logo, black trousers, and sturdy black leather shoes with chunky soles. Black hides the stains and the dirt really well (especially if you are a brown handed barista like me, with permanently coffee stained fingers). Black is also cool – I look like a café ninja!

I go downstairs and start to get my things together. I get the cloths out of the dryer and dump them into a milk crate – nice and clean for the many spills and splashes we'll have today. I collect my laptop and car keys and head for the car. It's a twenty-minute drive to the café which gives me some time to relax and to think about what other things I need to do. I must call the people to get the grease trap cleaned out and I must talk to the chef about changing over to a summer menu. I'm particularly excited about the new menu – we've got some beautiful dishes planned that I know will boost our reputation even further.

As I drive into the street where the café is I get a sudden surge of excitement. This happens to me every day. I'm lucky that I get to go to work and feel this way.

I had a day off yesterday and am thrilled to find that my supervisor has done a great job and that everything is in perfect order outside – the terrace has been freshly mopped and the windows are sparkling clean.

I arrive at the building and stop briefly to check my mailbox. I then drive through into the parking lot within the building and park in my spot just behind the café. The bread is waiting for me at the back door. We have a great bread supplier and I trust him with a key to the complex so he can deliver our bread safely.

I open the back security gate, open the café door and switch off the alarm. Sometimes I wonder if I should set it off on purpose to wake up the neighbours and boost the morning coffee sales! But today I switch it off and I bundle down the stairs into the hot, musty café, dump my cloths and bread and start on getting everything set up.

The first thing I do is to scan the café to make sure everything is in place. I love everything to be tidy and in its place (even when we are closed) so that when customers walk by and look in the windows they know that they are looking at a clean, professional operation. The next thing I do is to switch on my beloved coffee machine. I treat it like an old friend and I look after it with love! It takes about fifteen minutes before the steam starts to build up and about thirty minutes before it is ready to be used, so I have to switch it on as soon as I get there.

Next I assemble the dishwasher and switch on the plumbing tap (I switch it off every night just to be on the safe side). Every day at close-up the dishwasher is disassembled and cleaned so it needs to be put back together and filled with powder before the start of the day. Again, it takes some time to warm up and be ready for use, so it is the second thing I switch on. I then set up some buckets filled with hot soapy water to soak the cutlery in before it goes into the dishwasher. This allows us to store dirty cutlery neatly when the dishwasher is running. It is also easier to wash all of the cutlery at once in the flat basket. I then fill up the small sink with hot, soapy water so that the pans can be soaked and washed prior to going in the dishwasher. It's important that the dishwashing area is well organised as we operate for the first three hours without a kitchen-hand (we share the dishwashing tasks on a weekday until 10:30 a.m. when the kitchen hand will arrive). This saves a few dollars when the café isn't overly busy. The negative side to this is that if we do get busy we start to get a backlog of dirty plates, but if we are well organised and work fast this doesn't occur.

While the coffee machine and dishwasher are warming up I start to set up the rest of the café. When I first bought the café the previous owner took me through everything and I wrote everything down and created step-by-step procedures. This now forms our operations manual which is a fantastic reference guide for all the staff in the café. I also use it to train my supervisors – particularly how to open and close up.

Next I set up the till. To do this I retrieve the till float and previous day's takings from my "secret" location inside the sugar bag in the dry store. Now, I don't recommend this to anyone but I found it was the best solution for a few reasons:

- It meant that my staff didn't have to walk home with large amounts of money in their pockets
- It meant that I could bank the money the next day
- The money was insured whilst "on the premises"
- Leaving the float at the café meant that I wouldn't accidentally leave it at home!

Once the float has been put in the till and I have safely stored the previous day's takings I set up the tables inside. First I take the chairs off the tables (we stack the inside ones at night). I then open up the doors and start setting up the outside area – making sure that I place a line of chairs across the opening of the café with our opening hours sign. I do this so that it is clear to customers that will be ready to open shortly – there are always a few early birds desperate to get in and have their morning coffee.

I continue to set up the café – tables, chairs, salt and pepper shakers (always in the same standard position on the tables), umbrellas (always set up the same way) and an A-frame chalkboard (with a promotion written on it). Once the tables are set up (15 minutes before opening) I go back in to get my coffee machine ready. I organise my section: cloths, spoons (for stirring sugar, making macchiatos, etc.) milk jugs, thermometers, sugar for take-away coffee, take-away cups, napkins, take-away bags, sliced lemons for soft drinks, strawberries for smoothies. I also then pick up the daily newspapers (conveniently hidden in the bush at the front door) so that our customers can enjoy reading them with their morning coffee.

I fill up the empty grinder with a bag of fresh beans and savour the aroma whilst I flick the switch for a few seconds. I let the grinder run until I have got enough for a couple of shots. I dose, tamp, rinse the group head and lock in the shot. It's good but not perfect so I adjust the grind again to get it spot on. I time the shot until I get close to a 25 second extraction. It starts to spiral beautifully as it pours and I know I've got a killer espresso extraction. I flick the grinder back on and let it fill up. I'll continue to adjust the grind gradually throughout the day as the weather changes and the beans start to sweat, but I'm safe to fill up the grinder as I know I'll use all the ground coffee quickly. Purists may grind to order – and that's fine – but the acoustics of my café mean that it's not great for customers to listen to a continual rat-a-tat of grinding and dosing to order.

I flick on the grill and the toaster at 7:20 a.m. – they take a bit of time to heat up and the chef likes them to be ready when he walks in a few minutes before opening. This means that if customers turn up at 7:30 a.m. on the dot we are ready to start cooking straight away. At that time of the morning customers need a speedy turnaround and we have to be ready to give it to them.

I then set up my laptop on one of the bigger tables so I can do some paperwork if we aren't too busy.

So, we're all set up and I only need one thing – staff! I

recruit staff who are flexible with shifts so that I have adequate cover in all situations – this means that I have plenty of options which makes it easier to organise the weekly roster.

"Good Morning!" says my smallgoods supplier as he squeezes in the door. He hands me a docket which I quickly check and sign and I dump the large boxes of bacon, sausages, sliced ham and roast turkey on the counter for Chef to sort out once he arrives. I make my smallgoods man an espresso which he takes away with him. This reminds me to make one for myself – after all, one must test the product!

Chef then comes ambling across the road and gives me a "How ya goin' matey?" He's relaxed, calm and organised. A good chef will always be organised, but one that is calm and relaxed is a real asset. I've never seen him get stressed – just busy.

He immediately starts setting up his *mise-en-place.* That's a fancy French term for getting everything that he needs to do his job organised. It's got to all be there in abundance. If we are short of any ingredients chef will start prepping them immediately whilst he gets his pans of hot water organised for the many beautiful poached eggs he will serve today.

I have a few minutes to enjoy my cappuccino and look

out onto the street – and as I do so the waitress arrives. She's dressed in black, hair pulled back, sensible shoes and happy to be here. She is one of my student waitresses, many of which live close to the nearby university. It's a great source of staff particularly as they are mostly intelligent and mostly poor – an ideal combination for a café! They also have a free job posting service on the university website. Free is good.

I sip my cappuccino whilst the waitress and the chef banter to each other as she gets her apron and her docket books and pens organised. I ask Chef, "Ready to go?"

"Bring it on!" he says and the waitress trots out to put the outside chairs in place and to open the two big front doors. She also pops the umbrellas up and as she's doing so the first of our regulars pass her by with a cheery "Hello". Most of my regulars will have the same drink or food every time they visit – regular as clockwork. And with that the waitress passes me the dockets for our first sit-in orders of the day and my regular take-away customers start to form an orderly queue at the counter whilst the waitress dashes back and forth controlling both the floor and the till. She's been with me for a year so she's a great asset – fast on the floor and knows exactly when to pop behind the counter to help out with take-away orders and the till. Working with her is a joy – I tell her that working together we are "the dream team" and I can tell that she loves hearing me say that (so I say it often). Anyway, we're off and running and before I know it things are starting to get really busy...

In every café there is a period of morning madness called the coffee rush. It will hit sometime before 9am, but it varies every day. It's a short period of time where a critical mass hits and it's all hands to the pump. It's a challenge, but an enjoyable one. It's a critical period of time as these people are your regulars – the types that get the same coffee every day. They are our bread and butter. Some I know by name – all of them I know by their coffee orders. Sometimes I see them coming and I have their coffee made before they even walk in. They love that! There isn't so much of a coffee rush on the weekend but when it hits during the week and it combines with an unusually busy eat-in crowd it can be really busy – but busy for orders equals a busy till! We ensure that we prioritise take-away orders over sit-in customers as sit-in customers are generally happy to relax over breakfast whereas take-away customers are watching the clock.

By about 10:30-11:00 a.m. the kitchen-hand arrives. She immediately gets stuck into the dishes and receives her prep instructions from the chef. He starts pulling out boxes of vegetables for her to chop and soon they are both like a mini production line, chopping everything from eggplants to bocconcini in preparation for lunch. They don't stop.

At this point I can relax a bit, stock up my bar, fill up the takeaway cups, napkins, adjust the grinder. Maybe even make myself another coffee. I have a chat to the chef and the waitress and get the waitress's lunch organised. I usually give them a sandwich – I let them pick. I even let them have a juice or a coffee. I'm such a nice boss! While the waitress sits and has her half-hour break the other deliveries start to arrive. During this time I work the floor and make coffee orders and do till all at the same time. It means that I have to be super-efficient at everything. Luckily I am! But if I start to get too busy I have to shout to the waitress to give me a hand. I don't like doing that but sometimes it's necessary.

A veritable symphony of goods then starts to trundle in – three crates of eggs, bundles of cheese, napkins, drums of oil, kilos of chicken, docket books. It all arrives and is carted away by me and Chef before the customers can set their eyes on it. I made a decision very early on that I would order everything in and this works well for me – I'd rather spend my time doing work that can help to build up the café rather than spending time running around buying stock. I also made the decision very early only to deal with suppliers who offered credit terms so that I could pay weekly – thereby saving time by doing all my payments at the one time once a week. Until then I keep all my invoices neatly inside the till to be taken home at the end of the day.

About 11:30 a.m. Chef will start setting up his *mise-en-place* for lunch. We sometimes get people asking for lunch at 11:30 a.m., even though we don't start serving it until 12:00 noon – but if Chef is ready we'll provide it if a customer asks. About 12:00 the main rush will start to happen. Unlike the coffee rush it is focused more on the floor than on the coffee – so I will try to get out from behind the machine to help the waitress if I can. If I'm honest I don't really like doing the floor, but it's part and parcel of being a café owner. I'd much rather be producing beautiful coffees.

Lunch comes and goes with the peak being between 12:00 and 2:00 p.m. After 2:00 p.m. I get a chance to sit down at a table and plug my laptop in and do some paperwork – I do this on a daily basis so that I don't have to do it at home. I feel that it's important to try to keep home and work separate, and so far I've been very successful at doing that. I sit myself on a table and do my work: pay invoices, arrange staff rosters and place orders. When I order stock I use a laminated checklist in which we write down quantities of stock in erasable marker pen. I also have a laminated supplier list which has contact details on it for quick reference. We have approximately 20 suppliers so it pays to be organised.

At 3 p.m. we close down the kitchen. Sometimes we get a few customers coming in just after 3 p.m. – we'll usually serve them if they ask for lunch, but after about 3:10 p.m. it isn't worth paying the chef an extra half hour to feed a couple of people. At this point the chef will start his close down. He will put away all ingredients, give all pots and pans to the kitchen hand to clean, wipe down his areas, switch off all appliances, clean the hot plate and burners lightly. Once a week the chef will do a "full" clean which will involve removing all the burners and wiping down the walls around the stove. Once a month we clean out the oil that collects in the range hood. I am always careful to do this as another local café had gone on fire because the range hood hadn't been cleaned. I pride myself upon the cleanliness of my beautiful café.

Once Chef has cleaned up he's out the door like a flash – but just before he leaves he completes his preparation list for the next day and pins it up to start on tomorrow. At this point we also start to close up. This involves bringing in the umbrellas, advertising sign, ashtrays and salt and pepper shakers as well as stocking up the bar. If there are no customers inside we will wipe down all the tables and start stacking the chairs inside (we leave the outdoor area open until 3:30 p.m.). At 3:30 p.m. I put a sign on a chair outside that says we are closed and I shut the doors until we are ready to clean the outdoor patio.

After I wipe down all the tables the kitchen hand finishes cleaning the dishwashing area and disassembles the dishwasher. I then stack all the tables and chairs and the kitchen hand sweeps and mops the floor inside and out. Whilst she does this I clean out the grinder and coffee machine. I use the leftover ground coffee to make espresso for iced coffees then I make up the chocolate mix to use for mochas and iced chocolates. I also check I have enough lemons, strawberries, take-away coffee cups, stirrers, sugar, etc. so that I will be ready to hit the ground running come 7:30 a.m. tomorrow.

After that I cash up (always with the exterior door locked for security). My Eftpos machine would settle automatically overnight but the till has to be cashed up and settled at the end of each day. I run my X reads, check all my totals, balance the takings and then do my Z reads to clear the totals. Wow – another great day! It gives me one final surge of excitement! I place the cash in an express deposit bag which I will take home and drop off at the bank later in the week. The float will then go back to its magic hiding place.

The next thing I do is carry the bin down the stairs into the café and then lift the full bin bag out of the kitchen bin and into the outside bin. I also gather up the cardboard and stack it outside beside the bin. Finally after the kitchen hand is finished I say goodbye to her and throw the last of the dirty cloths into a milk crate. I check the outside area for anything left and then lock the door. Next I go around and make sure all the sockets and stoves are off and that everything is clean. If it isn't I give it a quick buff with a cloth.

So finally the café is clean and silent, I climb the stairs to the car park and I look over it for a few seconds and feel a swelling of pride – it's clean, shiny and ready for another busy day tomorrow. *This is my café.* I have created a thriving business through a lot of hard work and it has paid off.

I have my bag of money and my crates of cloths. If I am not working the next day I write notes on the whiteboard for my supervisors and then I carry my crates and money out through the back door and load them into the car. I leave the float in the secret hiding place, switch the lights off and the alarm on and lock the doors behind me. I jump into the car and out of the parking lot at 5:00 p.m. and my day as a café owner is done.

A Day In The Life Of A Café Owner

About Craig Reid, The Café Ninja

Craig Reid is one of Australia's top business improvement consultants and is a former owner of one of Sydney's most successful breakfast cafés. His no-nonsense, practical advice has helped businesses big and small to improve without costing them an arm and a leg – critical in today's tough economic times.

Craig holds postgraduate qualifications in Hospitality Management, an honours degree in Marketing and his experiences as a chef, barista, café owner, waiter and even dishpig have given him a complete end-to-end perspective on running cafés.

Craig has also been a reviewer for *"The Coffee Guide… Sydney"*, a writer for *Flyingsolo.com.au*, and has been featured on *BNet Australia*, as well as in the entrepreneur section of *The Australian* newspaper.

Need help buying, starting or running a café?

Contact

craig@thecafeninja.com

www.thecafeninja.com

www.ingramcontent.com/pod-product-compliance
Lightning Source LLC
Chambersburg PA
CBHW021858230426
43671CB00006B/437